# Reaching *beyond* the Pain

### FINDING JOY IN THE MIDST OF SUFFERING

"Are you overcome with pain? Searching for hope? Wondering where true healing can be found in the midst of great suffering? Then, *Reaching Beyond the Pain* is a must-read for you. In her book, Diana Shafe puts together a collection of real-life stories from people who have experienced unthinkable hardship, yet found hope and healing through one common denominator—Jesus Christ. As you read this book, there is no doubt that you will experience God's power, find comfort in His beautiful presence, and be encouraged to trust in Jesus because as you'll see, He truly cares for you."

— REV. JASON ENGLE
Lead Pastor
Jackson Free Methodist Church

"In *Reaching Beyond the Pain*, Diana Shafe has brought together a collection of moving Christian testimonies about dealing with trauma that might otherwise have been overlooked. The variety of its contributors is evidence of the universality of suffering and the ability of people to speak meaningfully about their experience. Reading these accounts will reinforce our fellowship in the Holy Spirit as He reminds us of how we are united by glorifying the Master of suffering together."

— ELTON D. HIGGS, PH.D
Emeritus Professor of English
University of Michigan-Dearborn

# Reaching *beyond* the Pain

### Finding Joy in the Midst of Suffering

## Diana Shafe

*Reaching Beyond the Pain*
by Diana Shafe
reachingbeyondpain@gmail.com.

Copyright © 2025 Diana Shafe
All rights reserved.

Printed in the United States of America
ISBN: 978-1-962802-41-3

All rights reserved. Except in the case of brief quotations embodied in critical articles and reviews, no portion of this book may be reproduced, stored in a retrieval system, or transmitted in any form or by any means—electronic, mechanical, photocopy, recording, scanning, or other—without prior written permission from the author.

This work depicts actual events in the life of the author as truthfully as recollection permits and/or can be verified by research. Occasionally, dialogue consistent with the character or nature of the person speaking has been supplemented. All persons within are actual individuals; there are no composite characters.

Unless otherwise stated, all scripture is from Life Application Study Bible, NIV. 2007, Tyndale House Publishers, Inc., Carol Stream, Ill.

Scripture quotations marked NIV are taken from THE HOLY BIBLE, NEW INTERNATIONAL VERSION®, NIV® Copyright © 1973, 1978, 1984, 2011 by Biblica, Inc.® Used by permission. All rights reserved worldwide.

High Bridge Books titles may be purchased in bulk for educational, business, fundraising, or sales promotional use. For information, please contact High Bridge Books via www.HighBridgeBooks.com/contact.

Published in Houston, Texas, by High Bridge Books.

# Dedication

One person has consistently lifted me up, stood by my side, and embodied one of the greatest blessings in my life—my dearest friend and unwavering supporter! My husband Steve.

Furthermore, I also wish to dedicate this entire book to my five cherished grandchildren, who provide me with profound joy simply through their presence. It is my sincere prayer that they will always recognize and comprehend the true source of authentic, genuine joy throughout their lives, regardless of the challenges they may encounter along the way!

# Contents

| | |
|---|---|
| FORWARD | XIII |
| Reflections from Diana | 1 |
|    Introduction | 3 |
|    1. Loss of Innocence | 7 |
|    2. Victim to Victory | 17 |
|    3. An Amazing Life | 27 |
|    4. Hope Deferred | 41 |
| Reflections from Others | 47 |
|    5. Forgiveness | 49 |
|    6. Broken Promises | 55 |
|    7. Second Chances | 61 |
|    8. Set Free | 69 |
|    9. Shattered Dreams | 79 |
|    10. Walking in Faith | 87 |
| Reflections on Grief | 93 |
|    11. Love and Loss | 95 |
|    12. Emily's Story For His Glory | 101 |

| | |
|---|---:|
| Final Reflections | 139 |
|    13. Closing Thoughts | 141 |
|    14. Encouraging Words | 145 |

# Acknowledgements

I cannot thank Dr. Elton and Dr. Laquita Higgs enough for their unwavering encouragement and meticulous scholarly editing. Their guidance has been invaluable. I can't imagine completing this book without them. I am deeply grateful for the profound and meaningful friendship that we have developed. They are true treasures in my life that I will always hold dear.

Dr. Vicki Kloosterhouse, what can I say about someone who has been a friend for almost fifty years? She has been an incredible inspiration and has relentlessly encouraged me to write my story for many years. So here it is, finally! Completing this work is a clear testimony to the depth of my respect for her and our shared love for Jesus.

Thank you also to each of the individuals who humbly accepted my invitation to share their story. Their willingness to revisit the pain in their past was clearly motivated by their desire to honor Christ and help others find joy even when dealing with pain. It has been my privilege to grow closer to each of them as they granted me access into their lives.

# Forward

I have known Diana for over 40 years. We met through my husband, a retired State Police officer, whom Diana wrote about in Chapter 2. I've watched her walk through many of the experiences she shares in this book. It's hard to fathom how one person could endure so much. And honestly, what she writes about is only part of her story—there's even more she has faced.

There were times when I didn't know if she would make it through. I often found myself asking God, "Why? Why does one woman have to bear so much pain and hardship?" Yet again and again, I've been amazed by her resilience, grace, and steadfast trust in the Lord. I've seen her reach out to comfort others walking through similar trials, and now, through this book, she is extending that compassion even further. Perhaps this book is part of the answer to my "why"—God is using her suffering to encourage and bring hope to others.

In these pages, Diana shares not only her journey but also the stories of others—stories of brokenness, forgiveness, shattered dreams, and loss. A common thread runs through them all: It is only by the hope and grace of Christ that any of them have been able to weather life's storms.

I'm deeply grateful for the hope these stories offer. We all face trials, and through the words of Diana and others, we are reminded that there is a way forward—one lit by faith, perseverance, and God's unwavering love.

**—Vicki Kloosterhouse, PhD**
   Author of *Un-de-terred: Embracing Our Purpose, Facing Our Challenges*

# Reflections from Diana

# Introduction

This project has been incubating in my heart and mind for decades, 25 to 30 years. Whenever I faced a new challenge or heartache, I felt an increased sense of responsibility to share my story. Over the years, I have taken small steps by speaking to many women's groups and through countless one-on-one conversations. However, I still had a desire to do more. Eventually, as my husband and I transitioned into a new season of life, I became increasingly sensitive to the stories of those around me, and my vision for this book expanded to include others who were also "reaching beyond the pain."

It has been my privilege to interact personally with each person who has contributed to this book, and I have been blessed to observe firsthand their joy even when their journey involved deep pain and loss. As I reflect upon our collective stories, I see a common thread captured by a verse from the Gospel of John. "I have told you these things so that in me you will have peace. In this world, you will have trouble. But take heart! I have overcome the world" (John 16:33).

This text conveys two essential truths: First, we will all face difficulties in this life. Everyone has a story, and that story will inevitably reflect some measure of pain and sadness, which is why it is so important that we approach one another with empathy and compassion. Second, when trouble and pain come, we can each have hope because Christ has overcome the world and offers His peace to us.

Each contributor to this work has reached beyond personal pain because they consciously chose to embrace a real and personal relationship with Jesus Christ as their Lord and Savior.

Their faith in Him and His presence in their lives have been a sustaining force as they have faced very difficult challenges.

This is not a book solely based on my personal circumstances, although I have written about a few of them. We, the authors of these writings, have found a way to reach beyond the immediate pain and suffering to something greater, filling ourselves with gratitude and deep-seated joy. We are aware that pain comes to us in many forms, from childhood scars to the immediate physical pain you may be trying to endure at this moment.

We have struggled with the pain of child sexual abuse, infertility, assault, amputations, divorce, addiction, loss of loved ones, disabled children, and the death of a child. We have all experienced real pain in these situations, yet we have found our way to not only survive but also to live with genuine joy, even in the most challenging of circumstances.

We desire this book to encourage you and bring new hope to your situation, to reclaim lost joy in your life again. We have been praying that we will clearly describe our purpose in each chapter in such a way that, by the time you have finished reading, you will be prepared to reach beyond any circumstance you might face in your life. If an experience has stolen your joy, may you find genuine joy, as we have, by "reaching beyond your pain."

Introduction

It has not been easy for us authors; each of us has endured the anguish of reliving our challenging experiences during the writing process, but we have agreed to share our painful journeys in the hope of helping others. We will not promise you miraculous healings, although that may happen, and we can't promise joy because that is something you must be willing to choose for yourself. However, we are confident this book will show you how to find the opportunities and strength if you decide to "reach beyond the pain."

As you read the many stories in this book, may they reveal how God has helped each author find genuine joy in their lives. May they encourage you to seek a relationship with God that will help you grow closer to Him so that you, too, may know genuine joy!

# 1

# Loss of Innocence

As a wise superintendent said, "Being nice includes more than just being polite; it also includes having empathy for those around you."[1] As another word of advice states, "Be kind, for everyone you meet is fighting a battle you know nothing about."[2]

As an adult, I have a special place in my heart for children! Children count on adults to protect them from evil, yet that doesn't always happen.

I had loving parents who had my sisters' and my best interests at heart. Unfortunately, through no fault of their own, my parents' best intentions didn't always provide the protection they desired.

When I was a three-year-old child, sexual abuse entered my life. My parents had no idea that this was happening to me. My grandfather was a sexual predator. I found out later in life that he had victimized multiple children. Yet, he did his best to hide what a terrible person he was.

No matter how often I asked for the abuse to stop, the threat was always that if it weren't me, it would have to be one of my sisters, and if I dared to tell anyone, terrible things would happen to me and my family.

As a child, I had no idea what those terrible things would be, but I was too scared to find out; therefore, I remained a silent victim, as so many do. I remember sleeping with my grandmother in her bedroom, and I would toss and turn and even cough loudly, hoping to wake her before my grandfather came in to get me. However, that was useless because she usually slept until noon every day. When he came into her bedroom, I would pretend I was still sleeping, and he still would make me get up early with him.

Often, when I had to stay with my grandparents, I would try to hide from my grandfather in the fruit cellar, which was located in their basement. However, my fear of their basement was nothing compared to my fear of my grandfather. My abuse continued with great frequency until I was about thirteen years old. The abuse ended when I became pregnant.

Fortunately, I had a miscarriage, although it wasn't until I was older that I realized what had happened to me. While in my ninth-grade class, I took a trip to the museums in Chicago. As I was looking at the jars of fetuses in various stages, it was then that I realized what had happened to me at thirteen. As I looked at the two-month fetus, I then understood that what I had experienced was a miscarriage.

The shame that it caused me affected every part of my life. As an adult, I sought out counseling to help me deal with the abuse so that it would have less of an effect on my life later.

I spent the majority of my young life trying hard not to let others know the emotional pain I was dealing with in my life. I attempted to mask my heartache through my involvement in various activities and accomplishments.

A friend in junior high school wanted to become a cheerleader. She was confident she would be selected and said, "Don't worry if you don't make it, because it really isn't that big of a deal; I would just feel better if you tried out with me." I was most concerned about my friend's rejection, so I agreed to try out with her. I was so nervous that I worked diligently to practice for the tryouts. Ironically, I was selected, and she was not. Our friendship didn't go well after that. So much for it not being a big deal, but it put me on a path of achievement. I also began dance lessons and probably worked harder than other dancers or cheerleaders. My accomplishments in these areas were an early source of false confidence and encouragement.

As it turned out, I was the only one chosen to be a cheerleader for all four years of high school, but I was never captain. I was also successful in my dance career, for my dance instructor insisted that I enter the Miss Battle Creek pageant, which I desperately didn't want to do. Amazingly, I became the first runner-up, missing the title by only one point, and received a college scholarship. However, if I had earned two more points, I could have won.

Even with the many other successes I had experienced, my abuse overshadowed so many of my thoughts that I never felt good enough for anything.

All of this changed when I married my high school sweetheart, Steve, and shortly afterward, the most amazing thing happened in our lives. Karon, a co-worker, kept inviting me to church. I wasn't interested in attending a church service, but she said they were having a great concert. Thinking that would be "safe," I accepted the invitation. Then, another person from work heard that I was going with our mutual co-worker and asked, "Do you know what they do at that church?" I didn't have any idea. She proceeded to tell me that they have "altar calls."

"What is an altar call?" I asked. This person had no idea but said that all she knew was that people go down to the front of the church crying and praying. She said they make a crazy scene.

Oh, no! I needed to warn Steve because I felt like he definitely wasn't up for anything like that!

The day of the concert came, and Steve and I were sitting in the parking lot; I thought this might be the right time to tell him about the altar calls. He gave me a disconcerting look, and then I promised him, "Sweetheart, no matter what, if we are the only two people left sitting, I will stay with you."

I don't know if my friend and her husband planned it, but they sat between Steve and me. The lights went down, and the concert began. It was amazing! The singer shared a scripture from Romans 3:23: "For all have sinned and fall short of the glory of God."

There was no question that that applied to me; I was sure I was full of sin, especially from all the abuse I had endured, and we were invited to accept Jesus Christ as our Savior. We were instructed to go to the altar to pray. It was very dark in the room, and we could not see each other, so I didn't know if Steve went down first or if I did. We were both unaware that the other had gone down front. When the lights came on, Steve and I were standing right next to each other. I thought he came down for me, and he thought I had gone down for him.

This was the evening that our life trajectory changed forever!

When I prayed to receive Jesus Christ into my life, I also prayed for Him to cleanse me from all of the filth (sin) that the sexual abuse had put upon me. I know that praying for cleansing doesn't always give immediate results, and my journey to complete healing is ongoing as I continue to read God's Word.

However, I can tell you that when I stood up after praying that prayer, I felt an overwhelming sense of cleansing that I had never experienced before. I was determined to learn as much as possible about what Jesus would do for anyone willing to reach out to Him; I realized that we need to confess our sins and recognize that Jesus died for our sins and was raised three days later, then we need to ask him to come into our hearts and lives. He will. I've seen it happen in so many people. The following are the Lord's words to us.

> Here I am! I stand at the door and knock. If anyone hears my voice and opens the door, I will come in and be with Him, and he with me. (Rev. 3:20)

This is all required to begin a sincere relationship with Jesus Christ. I also strongly recommend attending a Bible-preaching church to support you on your spiritual journey toward full recovery.

Both Steve and I realized that we needed the love, peace, and joy that only Jesus could give us, and we both freely received Jesus Christ as our personal Savior.

As we all returned to our seats, the singer, Dave Boyer, said, "Acts 2:21 says, 'Everyone who calls on the name of the Lord will be saved.'" He wanted us to know this scripture is true for anyone who prayed the prayers we had just prayed.

Steve and I, without hesitation, knew wholeheartedly that he was telling us the truth, and we both felt a profound sense of peace. Afterward, we sat in our car for almost two hours, discussing the changes that needed to take place in our lives.

Our salvation began on February 29, 1976. One of the first changes in our lives was getting involved in a couple of intense

Bible studies. We started to grow spiritually like a whirlwind; neither of us could learn fast enough.

Fortunately, Karon and her husband, Doug, played a pivotal part in our lives from that point on. As our friendship with this couple and our relationship with Christ grew, Steve, who was studying to be a psychologist, eventually began to sense that God was leading him to pursue a career in vocational ministry.

I soon came to realize that, like many of life's challenges, recovering from my abuse would be a lifelong process. As I began to study God's Word and accept that it was written for me, I realized that Christ died to heal me from the shame I had held onto for so many years. It was increasingly freeing to embrace the truth that Christ died not only for the sins I may have committed but also to release me from the guilt I suffered as a victim.

Later, when the grandfather who had abused me as a child was in the hospital dying, I happened to attend a speaker training conference. During a break, the speaker approached me and said, "I can tell that you have an important story to share. Be sure to ask for permission from anyone affected by it first." I took this as a direction from the Lord to go see my grandfather. Once I got home, I explained to my husband that I needed to go to the hospital and address my grandfather. He agreed, hugged me, and said he would pray for me.

When I got to the hospital, my grandfather was in a deep coma. He was lying on a sand bed, which put the metal edge of the bed at chest height to me.

He was lying with his hands across his chest and appeared to be completely unresponsive. In a very low voice, I told him, "I have just come from a speaker's conference, and I was told that if I planned on speaking about anything that involved other people, I should get their permission first." I said, "I am not here to get your permission. I just want to inform you that I will be teaching other victims like myself how Christ has healed me from the awful abuse that you put me through." I added, "I want you to give me a sign if you understand what I'm saying." He actually moved his hand from his chest and reached toward my side of his bed.

A nurse was standing just inside the door of his room, and I was surprised when she said, "Did you say something to him? I've never seen someone in his condition move on their own."

I responded, "Not really," even though I had. She then moved his hand back across his chest and left the room. When I thought that his nurse was gone, I stated firmly, "I am going to speak to anyone who was a victim like me because you have caused me and others so much pain and suffering with your sexual abuse. I want others to receive the healing I have received through Jesus Christ, and if you understand what I am saying, I expect you to be very clear in your gesture to me."

Then, with tears that rolled down his face, he moved his hand 16 inches to put it on top of mine, which was placed on the bed frame. Much to my surprise, the nurse had re-entered his room again. She touched my shoulder and said, "You must be very special to him because he is crying as he reaches for your hand, and I have never seen this before." I smiled at her and then left. I got my point across to him, went home, and told my husband what had happened.

In the years to come, I continued my training as a speaker and helped many women understand that the abuse they endured was not their fault, as most believed. I also received training through our social service department called Safe

Touch, a preschool curriculum that I presented to several schools in our area.

Anything I could do to help heal other victims helped bring more healing to my own life.

In my young life, it would have been helpful to be made aware of resources that could have helped me find a safe place to process my abuse. Therefore, I have decided to include information for anyone who needs help with their abuse or wishes to help others.

## SOME CURRENT STATISTICS ABOUT INCEST, SEXUAL ABUSE, OR ASSAULT

RAINN is the nation's largest anti-sexual violence organization and leading authority on sexual violence. It is a dynamic organization comprised of experts in victim services, public education, public policy, consulting services, and technology. The RAINN team works together to provide best-in-class services for survivors, informs and educates the nation about sexual violence, and improves the public policy and criminal justice response to sexual violence.

If you or someone you know has been sexually assaulted, help is available.

## NEED HELP?

Call 800-656-HOPE (4673) to be connected with a trained staff member from a sexual assault service provider in your area.

## How Does It Work?

When you call 800-656-HOPE (4673), you'll be routed to a local RAINN affiliate organization based on the first six digits of your phone number. Cell phone callers can also enter the ZIP code of their current location to more accurately locate the nearest sexual assault service provider.

According to the National Sexual Violence Resource Center (NSVRC), one in five women in the United States experience rape or attempted rape during their lifetime. Additionally, nearly 25% of men have experienced some form of sexual violence in their lifetime.[3]

Every 68 seconds, an American is sexually assaulted.[4]

The statistics mentioned are based on reported cases. The fact is that, much like my own experience and those of countless individuals I have talked with, the majority of men and women have never reported their abuse or molestation to any social service organization. This accentuates how pervasive this pain is and how many possible victims we interact with regularly.

Please don't hesitate to look for a counselor to help you process your pain. Please note that not all counselors are the same, and some may not be capable of meeting your needs. It took several meetings with different psychologists and counselors before I found one that I was comfortable with and who was able to meet my needs.

**RAINN** provides help through victim service programs to an average of 844 survivors daily.

**RAINN** is a national leader. As the nation's largest anti-sexual violence organization, it will give you any information you may need to help report and deal with molestation of any kind.[5]

Reaching *beyond* the Pain

A quick internet search for **RAINN** will lead you to a resource that helps answer any questions you may have.

Here are some suggestions for listening to or reading.

- I highly recommend Dr. Rick Hanson's reading materials, including his books and podcasts, which are available in bookstores and on Amazon.

- *The Sexual Healing Journey: A Guide for Survivors of Sexual Abuse, 3rd Edition* by Wendy Maltz. It is a highly respected resource for understanding and healing the intimate sexual problems caused by sexual abuse.

- *The Courage to Heal* by Ellen Bass and Laura Davis

- *Why Me? Help for Victims of Child Sexual Abuse* by Lynn Daugherty

May God bless you on your journey.

---

[1] John Denney, former Hanover/Horton Superintendent, Graduation commencement ceremony 2024

[2] Wendy Mass, *The Candymaker*: October 5, 2010

[3] The National Crime Victimization Survey (NCVS)

[4] Rape, Abuse & Incest National Network (RAINN)

[5] Rape, Abuse & Incest National Network (RAINN)

# 2

# Victim to Victory

Our salvation began on February 29, 1976. Our lives had taken a direction we would have never imagined possible. One of the most important scriptures I memorized in my first week as a new believer was from Hebrews 13:5-6, "'Never will I leave you; never will I forsake you.' So, we say with confidence, 'The Lord is my helper; I will not be afraid." What can man do to me?'"

Planning our wedding was an exciting time. However, I needed a better job, so I contacted an employment agency to expedite the process and spoke with one of their agents. She told me about a well-paying job, but I did not feel qualified for the position. She thought I should at least consider interviewing for this job. She said, "Don't be too concerned because this employer has a special employee training program." I asked her whether she knew how the program worked. She replied, "Although I don't have details, I know it has been very effective in training his employees." She went on to say, "I am also sending six other young women." So, I decided to go ahead and interview with this accountant. All seven women arrived at approximately the same time for the tests and the interview.

As I suspected, I had no idea how to operate the equipment required for this position. After taking the tests, we met with this accountant and business owner separately. I assumed that he had instructed each of us to return to the office at 4:30 p.m., where he would discuss the test results with us and inform us of his selection for the position. It didn't give me cause for concern because this office, which employed three other accountants and a receptionist, closed at 5:30 p.m.

I was unaware that he had requested that only I return at 4:30. He had a plan for me, and it required that the entire office be closed at 4:00 p.m. and that only he and I be there.

When I arrived at his office, he was on the telephone and told me to sit in one of the other offices. I thought it odd that the office was empty of all the other employees. As I sat down in one of the offices, I saw him lock the main door to the offices with a key, which meant there would be no way for me to open the door and leave. Terror raced through my heart!

Immediately, that scripture came to my mind, which I had memorized from Hebrews 13:5–6: "Never will I leave you; never will I forsake you. The Lord is my helper; I will not be afraid. What can man do to me?" *Well…*

Just as I finished thinking about that scripture, he came to the room where I was sitting. He told me, "Why don't you come into my office so we can discuss your test results?"

I asked him where the other office employees were, and he responded, "It has been a difficult day for them, so I sent them home early." I asked him for my test results, and he said, "They were terrible regarding the equipment."

I chuckled and told him, "I'm not surprised because I had never seen or used the equipment before."

I stood to leave, and he said, "Please sit down. I feel you will be a perfect fit for this job."

Shocked by his comment, I asked him, "What do you mean?"

He continued, "I have the ideal training program for new employees, which has worked for many years." I was very confused, and he made me feel very uncomfortable, but out of respect, I sat down to let him explain his program to me.

The accountant said, "Let me begin by telling you about most people I work for. These people specialize in organized crime. I help them with their finances, so they appear legal. These people are scary. I will refer to them as an "organized crime unit."

I said, "You're joking!"

He replied, "I want to clarify: I'm not joking; you must remember that."

He then said, "Getting back to the job opportunity, this is how it works. I will keep track of every mistake you make each week, and on every Friday, you must stay after work, and I will punish you for every mistake you have made. This will help to train you quickly to stop making mistakes."

I said, "*I don't think so,*" and I stood again to leave.

He approached me and said, "Oh, it starts now! I have many mistakes that you have made on these tests that you took earlier today, and you *must* be punished for them."

Despite all that I did or said, he proceeded for the next two and a half hours to assault me. The Lord was so good to me because, throughout the terrible treatment my body received, I felt as though my soul floated above the room, and I never felt anything!

It finally ended when the building custodian and his young son entered the main office door with their key. When they entered, I jumped up and went to the door. The custodian knew something was seriously wrong and asked, "What is happening?"

The perpetrator replied, "Oh, she's had a bad day, and I was trying to comfort her." I quickly ran to my car. He followed me, grabbed my car door, and said with a smirk on his face, "Don't forget the kind of people I work for; you would be wise not to tell anyone what we have been doing because if you do, bad things could happen to you or your loved ones."

My assailant had no idea that I had heard those exact words a long time ago when I was victimized as a child. However, when I received Christ, I was taught through His Word in 2 Corinthians 5:17: "If anyone is in Christ, he is a new creation; the old is gone, and the new has come." I was a new and different person; I was not about to be bound by threatening words again!

I didn't know what to do at that time, so I said nothing until the following day when my mother accidentally walked in on me as I was getting out of the shower; she was shocked when she saw my bruises. She talked with me and felt that I needed to go to the hospital to make sure I was okay.

Then, after my doctor saw what had happened to me, his eyes filled with tears, and he said, "What a sick man. You need to go to the police." There was a state police officer who attended our church, so I talked with him at the post. As I spoke with some of the other officers, they informed me that hundreds of victims had reported incidents involving this man.

Then, what they told me helped to make me more determined than ever to follow through with pressing charges against him. Other victims had reported their experiences with this man to the police, but they always dropped the charges, which meant there wasn't a legal record of what he had been doing. The police believed that he had threatened them so severely that they were too scared to follow through with their charges against him. The police told me that no matter how he threatened me, they would do everything in their power to keep me safe, and they kept their word.

After the assault, Steve and I had only three months until our wedding date, and we were determined not to let this situation stand in the way of our dream wedding. Our special day arrived, and it was a great day for us. We blocked out all that had happened. Our lives were finally on the path to all we had dreamed of.

In reality, however, the following events were not what we had dreamed of living. As it developed, the legal process spanned five long years, encompassing both the criminal and civil trials. During these five years, I suppose I was always on my assailant's mind because he continually found ways to mentally scare me out of continuing with the court cases.

These are just a few ways that he thought he would convince me to drop the court case:

He would call me late at night (Steve worked the night shift) and threaten that my husband might not make it home. He would also tell me that I had better keep my children close, or who knows what might happen to them?

One of my worst experiences was when we lived in the country and our daughters were playing in the sandbox. I went into the house for no more than a moment to get them some water. That night, after Steve had gone to work, this perpetrator called again and said, "I sure hope the next time you leave your girls in the sandbox, they will still be there when you go to get them!" How could he have seen them without my knowing it?

I knew it was a mind game, so at least I wasn't going to let him know he was winning.

Then, several nights later, our home was broken into while my husband was at work and our children and I were sleeping.

The radio was turned on at total volume! Our bedrooms were on opposite ends of the house. I jumped out of bed and started to run to our daughter's bedroom, and as I ran down the hall, I could see that the outside door by their bedroom was swinging open at two in the morning. I was terrified that he had taken our girls. Fortunately, our daughters were sound asleep.

He once saw me and our precious daughters at a large store. I didn't see him until he grabbed my cart and said, "You sure have beautiful girls." Then he chuckled and said, "They might be next!" He walked away as if there was no problem with what he had done. I was so terrified that he would do such a thing in front of my daughter that I left the store immediately.

So much for a speedy legal and civil process. After five years of his torturous antics, he was found guilty of criminal/sexual assault, and he ended up being offered a plea deal. Because my case against him was his first to go to trial, his punishment consisted of a mere $500.00 fine and three years of probation. The fortunate thing about our trial is that it was his first conviction.

The emotional trauma that I suffered was severe, and my husband and my doctor felt it would be beneficial for me to seek counseling to help me deal with the PTSD I was struggling with. It took several attempts to find a great counselor who could connect with me personally. Fortunately, I didn't give up on finding an excellent counselor. I went through counseling for a year with an excellent Christian psychologist who encouraged me to seek scripture. I would recommend to anyone who may be struggling with traumatic experiences to find a *Christian* counselor because I have found through personal experience that some counselors can cause more harm than good.

I dealt with not only this assault but also the shame I felt from being sexually abused as a child. I came to realize that Christ not only died for my sins but for any sins that others might put upon me, such as sexual abuse and assault.

I have spent 49 years dealing with memories from my earlier life experiences, but the most important scripture I remind myself of comes from Philippians 3:13–14. "But one thing I do: Forgetting what is behind and straining toward what is ahead, I press on toward the goal to win the prize for which God has called me heavenward in Christ Jesus."

In the book of Philippians, Paul states that our goal is to know Christ, to be like Christ, and to be all that Christ has in mind for us, according to God's Word. We all live with the tension of what we have been and what we can become. I have found that the more time I spend in God's Word and try to apply it to my life, the more peace and joy I experience daily.

I try to remember what the character David Rossi said in the TV show *Criminal Minds*: "Scars only reveal where we have been, not where we are going." I strive continually to face life without fear so that my scars only reflect my past, not my future.

Many years later, the individual who had assaulted me turned government witness against the attorney who represented him in the case I brought against him. This attorney was being prosecuted for his involvement in various organized criminal activities that he had been involved in for many years. My assailant was the accused attorney's accountant, so he had a great deal of evidence on this attorney. The defense thought that my testimony could possibly help discredit the accountant's testimony. Therefore, I received a subpoena to testify in federal court.

## Reaching *beyond* the Pain

I thought it would take a very short time to give my testimony. I told my best friend that if she went with me, we could go shopping afterward. Little did I realize that this complicated situation would become even more bizarre.

As we approached the large courthouse steps, we were surrounded by FBI agents and state police officers who recognized me and told me that I could be in possible danger. My assailant had stated (*on* the witness stand) that if he saw me, he would kill me! Yikes!

We were immediately taken to a private office to ensure our safety until it was time for me to testify. As we entered this office, the attorney on trial tried to shake my hand. I looked at him with disgust as he said, "Thank you for coming to my defense."

I told him, "I am not here to help you; I recall what you said about me at my trial." I told him, "By no means am I here to help your defense, but I had to come due to the subpoena." Then, I walked away from him to sit in the lounge.

As I sat down, a woman in the same area said, "You're Diana, aren't you?"

I smiled at her and said, "Yes, have I met you before?"

She was startled and said, "No, but do you know who you were talking to just now?"

I said, "Yes, he was the attorney for the man who assaulted me."

She said, "I know, but do you know he is one of our area's biggest organized crime leaders?"

I swallowed hard and said, "Well, I didn't know that!" I asked her why she was there, and she told me she had been subpoenaed, too. I asked her why.

She said, "I'm a prostitute who is often hired by the man who assaulted you. He flies in from out of state several times a month to see me. Not for sex, but he would pretend that I was you, and then he would beat me and say lots of things he wanted to say to you!" I told her I was sorry for all the pain she must have endured. She said, "It's no problem because I'm a single mom, and it is an easy $500.00 an hour." It broke my heart that anyone would have to tolerate such abuse for financial gain. She seemed like such a sweet woman.

I told her, "It must be tough to be a single mom."

We were finally taken from this office to the courthouse after several hours. We were told my assailant, who had finished his testimony, was on a plane back to the West Coast, so I was out of danger. We were only at the courthouse for maybe twenty minutes when the court was adjourned. I was going to have to come back the next day.

My friend Susie and I left for home since it was too late to shop. My friend started our conversation on the way home. Her first comment was, "I think Steve (my husband) will need to come with you tomorrow because this is a little too scary for me!" We laughed nervously.

I said, "I couldn't agree more." I thanked her immensely for going with me, as we both had a crazy story to share with our husbands.

At the end of this process of giving my testimony, we found out that agents of my assailant had tried to kidnap our daughters after school one day. My husband was sitting on our porch, and he noticed the out-of-state license plate on the car parked close to their school. When he saw this man get out of the car, Steve ran to stop whatever this man had in mind. He scared this man, who jumped back into his car and sped off. We were told to meet at the office where we were the day before, and two attorneys wanted us to ride with them to the courthouse. This strange story was capped off by being told by these two men from Boston, Massachusetts, representing this attorney on trial, "We were informed that [my assailant] had planned on your daughters being kidnapped, but Steve, obviously, you stopped that from happening. We have also canceled the hit that he had put out on you, Diana, and we are in a position to cancel any and all plans for harming you and your family." We were stunned, to say the least! God sometimes even uses wicked men to protect us. I was called to the witness stand and gave my testimony. My testimony was taken without complication, and then Steve and I left for home.

A few days later, I briefly caught the end of a news broadcast about the defendant who had subpoenaed me. Thankfully, my testimony didn't affect the outcome of this case. The defendant is in prison for a very long time, and I was told that my assailant moved to the West Coast (I'm sure to stay alive), and this situation has ended for us.

THANK YOU, LORD!

Please be sure that if you ever experience an assault of any kind, you will commit to prosecuting the perpetrator to the fullest extent of the law. That will help others commit to do the same. As I mentioned earlier, there were hundreds of previous victims before me from just this one man, but had all dropped charges against him.

Our police forces are skilled at protecting anyone in this situation, and I am very thankful for that. I can't help but wonder if even one of the other victims had been willing to file a claim and follow through with it, it would most likely have saved many others from being victims. Police are dependent on assault victims being willing to file a claim. This will be an aid to both law enforcement officers and future victims.

# 3

# An Amazing Life

As we begin our lives, we never know what experiences we will encounter. The level of joy we hope to experience is often tied to those special moments.

I have already discussed some of the traumatic events in my life. My being sexually abused as a child and the assault I experienced as a young adult, but life was not done, bringing me difficult situations that could have robbed me of a joy-filled life if I let them.

Medical difficulties began to establish a pattern in my life that required me to reach for something more stable than just being healthy. This is when I realized that God's Word had much to teach me about pain and suffering. It includes the stories of many individuals who turned to God when confronted with various afflictions.

It is easy to think that we have all the answers. In reality, only God knows exactly why things happen as they do, and we must submit to Him as our Sovereign. As you read the Bible, decide to trust God no matter what happens.

Throughout my challenges, I have consistently sought to align my life with God so that I can trust in the Lord for His peace regardless of my difficulties. I can honestly say that God has brought genuine joy into my life. I could sometimes experience this joy by leaning into His presence while enduring suffering. There were other times when God miraculously intervened, and the outcomes were vastly different from what we had anticipated.

As Steve and I began our marriage, we decided that developing a five-year plan would be a great way to start our lives together, keeping us aligned as we faced our future.

Well, that lasted about five months. Part of our plan was to complete our college education, secure good jobs, and start saving for our future before starting a family.

After five months of marriage, much to our surprise, I discovered I was pregnant with our first daughter. Wow, we were both in shock! I became violently ill with the pregnancy and had to postpone not only my college education but also the job that was meant to help out financially.

This was the beginning of a roller coaster of medical difficulties that has continued for most of our marriage. These unpredictable difficulties brought about several miracles. Let me explain.

## Miracle #1

I had to have an emergency cesarean section for our daughter's birth because she came into the world upside down and backward, and that was not the worst news.

Our daughter was born without her left hip socket. The doctors told us about all the surgeries that would confront her future life, and fear gripped our hearts. As new parents, we were somewhat relieved that she was fitted with a brace to stabilize her tiny leg before discharging her from the hospital.

We belonged to an amazing church; needless to say, we had many devoted friends who prayed faithfully with us.

I had to take our precious daughter to her orthopedic surgeon every two weeks so that they could do X-rays to follow up on how she was developing. I faithfully attended each appointment, and at her six-week check-up, something unimaginable happened. After the X-ray, her doctor and nurse had her in a room without me. Then, one by one, the other three surgeons were called to her room. Needless to say, I started to panic as I couldn't imagine what was going on.

Finally, I asked to go into the room where they were meeting. As I entered, I could see all four surgeons looking at her X-rays with their arms folded across their chests. I was shaking with fear. I asked what was wrong, and they told me to come and look at her X-rays with them.

They asked me if I could see anything unusual about them. I carefully looked at each weekly image through tearful eyes, and when I reached the current day, I said, "Oh! She finally has the hip socket we've been praying for!"

The doctors smiled at my ignorance because what I saw was not normal, and I didn't know that. They proceeded to tell me that bones don't develop like that. My doctor returned my baby to me and whispered, "I believe God has answered your prayers!" He then wrote "divine healing" across her file. It still brings tears to my eyes as I remember the unbelievable joy of that moment.

What an amazing miracle! We rejoiced with our family and church friends because God had answered our prayers!

## Miracle #2

Just a few weeks later, while we were still overwhelmed at how blessed we were, Steve became very ill. After many tests, his doctor told me that he believed it was the beginning of colon cancer.

We were so frightened because his mother died from cancer at the early age of 47, and his paternal grandmother had passed away with a similar diagnosis. He had the same oncologist his mother had had, and to say we were scared is a complete understatement. Steve went through many horrific tests and was then scheduled for a permanent colostomy. The morning that his surgery was scheduled, his oncologist came into the room and told us that he had been up all night and didn't feel that he could do the surgery without one more test.

Steve could barely imagine one more test, and tears filled his eyes as he asked to please skip the test and move forward with the surgery. However, his doctor insisted that that would not happen until another test was done that morning.

God once again chose to bless us with another miracle! When the test results came back, they showed that the area where the cancer was located was healed with no sign of abnormalities! How? Only God knows, but I can tell you that Steve has not had another problem since that day forty-eight years ago. Thank You, Lord!

So, life continued as we cared for and adored our beautiful new baby girl. A few months went by, and I began having the same symptoms I had with my first pregnancy. Yes, it was true; I was pregnant again. How could it be? My doctor was confident this new birth control would stop any pregnancy from happening. This is not part of our five-year plan, at least not yet.

I realize now that our plan was certainly not God's plan for us. What I have learned over the years is that His plans are *always* better than any plans we humans make. I had to have a hysterectomy just a couple of years later, and had I not had my daughters when I did, our five-year plan would have been too late for me to have children.

While I was five months pregnant, I was having horrific headaches, and one night, I had a terrible seizure. Steve came home from work and found me in the morning. He took me to the hospital, and after a week, the seizures had not stopped. This led to my transfer to the University Hospital, about an hour from our home, where I remained a patient for a month.

The doctors discovered that I had a brain tumor on the left side of my head. They suggested, since it was so early in my pregnancy, that we abort our baby, and then they could remove the tumor. We refused their suggestions. Then they tried to convince us to deliver our baby, stating that we were in the safest place to deliver an early pregnancy, and the answer once again was a firm "no, thank you!"

The plan now was that as soon as our baby was born, I would go to the Mayo Clinic for the surgery.

It was time for our first daughter's birthday, and I begged my doctors to let me go home. Finally, they were convinced that I was getting noticeably depressed, so they decided to let me go home from the hospital, but on strict bed rest.

A month passed, and the routine of strict bed rest was challenging for me as a mother with a one-year-old baby. Eventually, due to a combination of physical and emotional stress, I went into labor two months early.

Our second beautiful daughter was born just fourteen months after our first, and what an amazing gift she was. How thankful we were to have our precious daughters. However, due to her early delivery, she struggled desperately following her birth. She was immediately placed in the NICU and kept on oxygen.

Due to my surgical complications from her delivery, I had gone two days after her birth without being able to see her. Then, on a Sunday afternoon, her neonatal intensive care doctor contacted Steve to say that if we wanted to see our baby, it would have to be now because he did not expect her to live much longer due to her inability to breathe on her own.

I was in a great deal of pain, but of course, I had him take me upstairs immediately. When I entered the unit where they cared for her, I was amazed at how beautiful she was. Most babies born two months early have no hair, and our daughter had a tiny head, no larger than a tennis ball, with jet-black hair that was already an inch long. They had to shave her front hairline to insert an I/V in her tiny forehead.

When I saw her, she was struggling, twisting side to side, trying to pull all of the tubes off of her little body. That should have indicated what a spunky spitfire she would become later.

Her doctor told us that her struggle was making it difficult for her to get the oxygen that her tiny body needed.

I sat beside her, touched her little foot, and began talking to her. She immediately closed her eyes and sighed. I honestly thought she had died at that moment, but when I gasped, she jumped and opened her big, beautiful blue eyes. I realized she would relax and sleep if I talked to her and rubbed her hand or foot. It was incredible to see her in such a peaceful state.

I continued at her side for five hours. Our pastor came up and prayed with us over her. I told the Lord, "She is an amazing gift; if it is your will, Lord, not to let her live, I will try to cope with whatever your choice will be." I must admit that my last comment was, "But please let her live!"

After five hours of sitting with her, I became very dizzy and felt extremely nauseous, so I told Steve that I needed to go to my room for a few moments. We told her doctor I needed to lie down for a little while. He commented to us, "I will come and tell you when she passes away." I didn't want to leave her, but I was getting sicker by the minute.

## Miracle #3

I was lying in my room for about fifteen or twenty minutes when I heard our Korean-accented doctor get off the elevator and urgently say, "Where Diana Shafe?! Where is Diana Shafe?! I need to see her now!" I just knew our baby girl was gone!

Her doctor entered my room and excitedly said, "I not know what your God do—I not know what your God do!"

I said, "What do you mean?"

He told us, "After you left, I was working on your baby, and I realized that she could take a deep breath on her own. Then I turned off her oxygen, and she began breathing without it. I checked her oxygen intake, and I believe she will make it, much to my surprise!"

My delivery of our second daughter required a second cesarean section; my doctors discovered the following day that I had been hemorrhaging internally and needed emergency surgery at once. He explained to us that another pregnancy would be extremely dangerous for me. Therefore, it was decided that I would have to undergo an additional procedure to end my ability to have the large family I dreamed of.

Our baby was born two months early, yet she went home at ten days old, much to everyone's surprise, and she has been healthy ever since. What, another miracle?

I must say that I don't understand when and why God sends miracles. I believe it is entirely at His discretion. We have the privilege to ask for one, not demand one, anytime, but for whatever reason, we have had our share, and He wasn't done with us yet.

## Miracle #4

After our baby and I came home, I eventually went to the Mayo Clinic for treatment for the brain tumor. I took the results from all of my previous testing. I spent one week having many of the same tests repeated. As I sat down with the doctors, they explained that they had repeated all the tests that had been conducted at the university and were aware of the results. However, according to their testing, no tumor could be detected. I went home the next day with a clear diagnosis! No future problems.

My husband and I have often wondered why our lives have been filled with such a unique combination of challenges and blessings. While a definitive answer has been elusive, we have come to believe that the Lord wanted to get our attention and that He wanted us to realize precisely how real He truly is.

One significant result of these miraculous deliveries was a shift in Steve's career focus. Steve initially studied to become a psychologist. However, after accepting Christ, he concluded that providing people with psychological help was only addressing part of the issue. He realized he was being called into vocational ministry to guide people to spiritual healing that can only be found in embracing Jesus Christ as Lord and Savior. Upon receiving his undergraduate degree in psychology, he continued his studies and eventually became an ordained minister. His education has merged with our life experiences, equipping him to become an exceptional husband, father, and pastor.

I would love to tell you that all of my health problems have been resolved miraculously, but that has not been the case. The past forty-eight years have often been marked by significant suffering for Steve and me. I have had twenty-eight major surgeries, and I wish I could tell you that there has been no pain with them, but just the opposite is true. I have suffered from horrific pain, and Steve has frequently borne the unique burden that comes with being the caregiver for a loved one. However, the most miraculous thing about our story is that, through the presence and power of our relationship with Christ, we have been able to experience an amazing level of joy, whether the healing was instantaneous or delayed indefinitely.

At this point, it is tempting to offer specific details about my many surgeries, including the complications, pain, and suffering that came with most of them. However, I believe that my readers would be better served by simply acknowledging that, more often than not, my physical restoration did not occur quickly. In preparation for writing this chapter, I took the time to reflect on my extensive medical history. I came to realize that, as a result of struggles that often extended for years, I gradually began to notice some patterns in my life that helped me reach beyond the pain to experience joy in the face of my difficulties. Therefore, I would like to conclude this section by highlighting four general points that I have found helpful in the hope that others will also find them beneficial.

## Cultivate a Source of Hope That Can Transcend Circumstances.

My greatest and most enduring source of human support, though, has been my amazing husband. I thank the Lord that

He has blessed me with this man in my marriage! He is the most sensitive man I know. He consistently prioritizes the needs of others over his own. He has stood beside me through all the crazy situations we have lived through, and I couldn't imagine my life without him!

During all of these ridiculous health issues, I have grown more aware of the presence of our Lord Jesus Christ in my life. I can't imagine living this life without my relationship with the Lord. It saddens me when I think of people living without a real life-changing relationship with our God. Anyone who truly knows me can attest that, despite all the difficulties I have faced in my life, the Lord has helped me in a way that only His Spirit can, to live not a pain-free life, but a genuinely joy-filled one. For me, my personal faith as a follower of Jesus Christ has helped me focus on the power that our Lord can provide when life seems out of control.

If you are reading this and don't know how to begin a real life-changing relationship with Him, it starts with praying to God and confessing your need for Him. Revelation 3:20 says, "Here I am! I stand at the door and knock. If anyone hears my voice and opens the door, I will come in and eat with him, and he with me."

Another important consideration is to attend a Bible-preaching church where you can receive the Lord's teachings in a way that makes it easy to apply them in your daily life. Additionally, I cannot stress enough the importance of becoming involved in that church, allowing you to build relationships with other believers and support your newfound faith. My husband and I made this life-changing choice forty-nine years ago, and it was the best decision we have ever made.

It is so simple to begin a real relationship with Him. I don't mean just going to church occasionally. That is a lie that so many people believe is enough. He stands at your heart's door, genuinely waiting for you to choose to live your life with Him.

Spending time reading the Bible, praying, and listening to Christian music often helps me redirect my focus away from my struggles and onto the security that God is and has always been in powerful control.

I have also realized that when I find and memorize encouraging scripture, it focuses my mind on the hope that God's Word provides.

## Develop a Personal Support Team During Every Season of Life.

People move in and out of our lives throughout the years. We need to invest intentionally in the lives of others, building relationships based on mutual love, support, and availability.

We intentionally worked to develop healthy, encouraging relationships as we modeled what friends can do to support people in difficult circumstances. Consequently, they were available for us when we needed their support during difficult times.

Friends sometimes brought in meals for two weeks at a time when necessary. They helped with our laundry and childcare, which was greatly appreciated. We had small daughters, and it was a great relief to know that our friends gave them opportunities to play with their children, and I knew their needs were being met.

I encourage you to consider what kinds of encouragement would be a huge blessing to you and be sure to offer that encouragement to those around you. It has a way of circling back to you when needed.

Developing a church family is critical. I can't tell you how many times I have received encouraging cards, flowers, and small gifts to lift my spirits. And they seemed to always arrive at the most needed times. The best part of having an excellent relationship with other Christ believers is knowing that they constantly support us with their prayers.

## Relentlessly Seek Out the Right Professional Help for Each Challenge.

Over the years, I have been blessed by countless doctors and healthcare workers, men and women who were kind, compassionate, highly skilled, and tireless in their drive to help me. Unfortunately, I have also encountered individuals who were arrogant, insensitive, mean-spirited, insecure, and incompetent to the extent of malpractice.

It is so important that you never allow someone to push you into treatment or procedures you are not comfortable with. It would be best if you were always willing to change doctors or seek second opinions when you feel unsure about the treatment or the attitude you might receive from anyone involved in your treatment team.

## Always Be Prepared to Advocate for Yourself.

You are always your best advocate, and please don't allow anyone, regardless of their position, to intimidate you. You need to protect your body and your life. This could be considered an extension of my previous recommendation, but I believe it warrants separate consideration. Be open with your family and your entire healthcare team about your needs and desires regarding your healthcare. Never hesitate to ask questions and press for a complete understanding of all your options.

Don't back down with your insurance company if they deny your claims or reject treatment recommended by your medical providers. This seems to happen more often than I wish to believe. Always check your insurance company's information so that you are in a position to question your coverage if necessary; if there is a discrepancy, be sure to research your policy before contacting the company; don't be intimidated about calling your company with your questions and always be sure to be polite, as it genuinely does make a difference. It is also wise to carefully review all of your billing statements. Over the years, this has prevented us from paying for numerous procedures that were covered by our benefits.

With all these suggestions for handling difficult situations, the best strategy is to consider whether you are building a foundation in your life that prepares you for any challenges that may arise.

It has been our prayer that everyone who reads this book will take the necessary steps to make our Lord and Savior the center of their lives. Christ is the only one who can help you reach beyond your pain to find His amazing joy.

# 4

# Hope Deferred

This is my story of indescribable, continuous pain. For several years, I suffered from the pain of what my doctors believed was rheumatoid arthritis, though later, it was discovered that it was a rare form of hepatitis C, contracted through numerous blood transfusions I had received. Believing it was rheumatoid arthritis, I was sent to a rheumatologist, who, in turn, sent me to physical therapy.

The physical therapist decided that pool therapy would be the best place to start to relieve my joint pain. I was introduced to a therapy technician who, unfortunately, encouraged me to twist harder in the water in the first session than I was comfortable doing, resulting in a disc in my lower back literally exploding. That "explosion" lodged fragments into the sciatic nerve in my spine, and it was only a few minutes before I realized I had a serious problem.

I found myself in such indescribable pain that it would take the rheumatologist almost three months to determine the cause of the pain and my need for surgery. I was so anxious for the pain to be eliminated from my life that we went to the first neurosurgeon that the rheumatologist recommended.

The surgery was not as successful as we had hoped it would be. The surgeon removed only *some* of the disc fragments lodged in my sciatic nerves, but unfortunately, a great deal of scarring was left behind, causing an increase in my level of pain. We later learned, through consultation with other doctors, that excessive scarring can occur when a surgeon is hurried and careless. With that information, I recalled that the surgeon had said he was very busy but would squeeze my surgery into his busy schedule. Too late, we learned a painful lesson: It would have been wise to research our options more than we did. Not all surgeons are equally trained or equally competent.

Finally, at the eight-year mark of enduring intense pain, I can honestly say that I had reached the point where I could not take this pain any longer, and I insisted that we had to come up with something that could help me. We decided to go to the Mayo Clinic Pain Center, which gave me hope.

I stood in a room at the Mayo Clinic Pain Center, genuinely eager to hear what the clinic's head physician had to say regarding my case. He was evaluating my records from the previous surgery and eight years of various modalities of treatment that many doctors had performed in attempting to bring my pain under control.

My heart leaped with anticipation as he entered my room. I had high hopes that he might finally have a solution or procedure that we had not heard about or had already tried.

He stared at the floor for what seemed to be an eternity, then broke the silence with words I didn't want to hear: "I… am… so… sorry; there is nothing more that can be done for you." I was stunned. I tried to stay focused, but I burst into tears; I was crushed.

I told him I didn't understand and that this clinic was the last place I could find help. I pleaded with him to think of anything that might help me. Obviously, my desperation moved the doctor, but he truly had no idea what else to do. He said, "I am so sorry, but nothing is left to try."

Before leaving my room, I pleaded with him to tell me how I would know what to do next. He stated, "You should be your own best advocate and stay at your computer because you never know when a new treatment may become available." His final words were, "I'm truly sorry. Please don't give up! Feel free to call my office if you have any other questions."

As the doctor left the room, my husband held me close as I sobbed inconsolably. He knew my devastation; he had lovingly walked every step of this journey of excruciating pain with me, and there seemed to be no end in sight. As we left the hospital, I blurted out that it seemed so unfair. It wasn't even our fault—someone else had caused it, and we were left trying to cope with it.

When I think back on all the suffering that I personally have endured, not to mention all that my precious family has gone through, it grieves my heart. I realize how suffering changes people. I tried desperately to be as fun-loving as my heart wanted to be, but when you have such intense pain screaming at your body twenty-four hours a day, you can only fake it so long until sheer exhaustion wins out.

Back home, I coped the best I could, trying not to let my pain cause me to neglect my little girls. During the many hours I lay in bed because of the pain, I would try to make it fun for my daughters. Sometimes, I would give them special markers and huge catalogs, telling them to circle everything they wanted in the catalog. Then they would crawl into bed with me and show me all the special items. They would tell me why they thought their items were special to them. I loved it when we did this together.

I found it critical to grow my relationship with the Lord during these times. Still, it was extremely difficult for me to read because I couldn't focus my eyes. So, I listened to as many Christian broadcasts as possible, knowing that my spirit truly needed the Lord's encouragement to hang on.

The Lord has an amazing way of giving you a single scripture at a time to meditate on until it really sinks into your soul. I felt like the Lord was speaking to me during these times as if He had given me a specific word that made me feel His presence like no other time.

My suffering continued, and eventually, a friend suggested that I try the Michigan Brain and Spine Institute. She was a former patient there and was very confident that they could help me. Initially, Dr. Steven Swanson told me he was a very gentle surgeon; I didn't understand his statement, so I laughed and said, "You're planning on putting me to sleep, right?" He, in turn, laughed and told me that when someone does surgery, any area that is touched inside your body can cause scarring. His plan, he said, was to remove as much scar tissue as possible, as well as the remaining fragments of the disc that were pressing on the nerve. This seemed to help relieve most of the pain for a couple of years.

At the Spine Institute, I eventually met another specialist, Dr. Mark Fallahee, who chose to perform a bone dowel fusion. The relief was short-lived due to a fall I had soon after returning home. When I went back to see Dr. Fallahee due to my pain again, he decided to do a titanium rod fusion, believing it would help my pain substantially. He was right, and it brought relief for several years, but over time, the pain returned, and this really frightened me, for I had dealt with this for over twenty-four years. I wondered if this pain was ever going to end. Most recently, Dr. Fallahee did a second titanium rod fusion, which has *finally* brought an end to the pain. Praise God! I have had no back or sciatic nerve pain since that day, and it has been nearly ten years! This, to me, is nothing short of a miracle.

I am not a stranger to pain, and by this time in my life, there have been seasons when I was well acquainted with it twenty-four hours a day. I mentioned in the introduction that pain comes into our lives through many physical, emotional, and spiritual experiences. Each can have a devastating impact on lives. I know what I am talking about, for I have had the opportunity to experience all three. During these times, I sought the Lord to help me focus on growing my relationship with Him. I am amazed at how the Lord taught me so much about Him and His word.

In Isaiah 55:6, we read, "Seek the Lord while He may be found; call on Him while He is near." God isn't planning to move away from us, but we so often move far from Him. I realize that the more I read my Bible and seek the Lord through devotions, sermons, and constant prayer, the more my relationship with and understanding of the Lord will grow. Those long, long years of suffering drew me to God and became the foundation of growth in Him, enabling me to receive His gift of unbelievable peace and joy even when I was suffering.

# Reflections from Others

# 5

# Forgiveness

## ANONYMOUS

In the Bible, the Greek word translated as "forgiveness" literally means "to let go." For me, the process of letting go is deeply rooted in my Christian faith. Did you know that over half of the Old Testament and New Testament Bible is a historical narrative? It makes sense. God's work is shown through our lives and testimony. This is true as far back as Adam and Eve, and it is true of my story. God is always working for our good.

I grew up in a family "living below the poverty level." Growing up poor and being embarrassed about it increased my vulnerability early on. When all my friends were planning a senior spring break vacation, I knew I wouldn't have enough money, even with my earnings from my fast-food restaurant job.

Being eighteen, you create ways to obtain what you want. So, I found myself hitching rides to Daytona, Florida, and being content to sleep on the floor of friends. My parents weren't in support of the trip at all. They placed a note in my suitcase, saying, "You need to think more wisely about your choices."

Those words burned a hole in my soul when one of the nights in Daytona, a boy from our school found me on the floor sleeping and raped me… and all I could think of when he was on me was the words my parents had slipped in my suitcase: "You need to think more wisely about your choices."

I never told anyone for fifty-four years what happened to me that night because I believed with all of my mind that it was my fault. To compound the emotions of guilt, I found out a month later that I was pregnant.

No one tells you how to process being raped or to deal with finding out you have an unexpected teenage pregnancy, so you do anything to return to the "before" life. That "anything" for me was an abortion. The shame and guilt that come with abortion are devastating, so to survive, you "bury it."

But, somehow, in life, with such deep shame and guilt, you fall into the trap of thinking you deserve hardship. When you feel like you deserve the negative circumstances you are in, you cannot heal. So, in my life, that translated into hanging out with those people who are choosing drugs and drinking and, in my case, having an abusive husband.

Somewhere in my identity, I believed that was what I deserved. I functioned in life, ignored my pain, and covered it up superficially. The devil consumed me in subtle but devastating ways, devouring my joy, peace, rest, and strength, as well as my health, relationships, and thoughts.

> Be alert and of sober mind. Your enemy, the devil, prowls around like a roaring lion looking for someone to devour. (1 Peter 5:8)

## Forgiveness

Years later, as a mother of a sixteen-year-old, I received a phone call from the hospital that my daughter had been taken to the emergency room. I was not told her condition, only that "We have your daughter."

Shaking and disoriented, I found myself in the emergency room, where they took me to a room to see my daughter, who was not breathing on her own. I remember getting close to her face and telling her repeatedly, "You are safe now; I'm here. You are safe now."

I learned over the next few hours that she had been drugged and raped. The shut door to all my trauma flew wide open and poured out, but this time through my daughter.

My precious daughter had been taken from the shopping mall, drugged, raped, and left for dead. As a Christian now, I can look back and understand that God grieved and felt deep sadness for all that happened to my daughter that day, and He grieved and felt sadness for my own hardships. In the same way, He feels deep sadness for all of the difficulties that any of us go through.

I spent seven years in a valley of hate and anger after my daughter was a victim of a violent crime, coupled with the unresolved issues from my past. God never wanted me to sit in that valley; it was time wasted.

For those currently experiencing a dark place, most of us can heal with God's touch by forgiving ourselves or others who have wronged us. To forgive ourselves, we repent, with full honesty, regarding both our sins and God's willingness to forgive and heal.

When we truly and wholeheartedly believe that God loves us, the gravity of Jesus dying on the cross for each of us is almost too overwhelming for our hearts. There is an ache in our spirits at the magnitude and the truth of Jesus' death, which enables us to be reconciled with our heavenly Father.

If we dismiss this truth and continue to decide that we are unforgivable, we dishonor all that Jesus did on our behalf. When we embrace the magnitude of what Jesus did in dying for our sins, we will be willing to lay down our shame and embrace freedom through forgiving ourselves.

Forgiving others for the harm they have inflicted on us or our loved ones is not saying you agree or think what someone did is all right. Instead, you are surrendering the person and wrongdoing to God. You are not giving up but giving over that which is stealing your energy and your joy by taking up space in your heart and mind. And when that wound is removed, there is more space for Jesus!

In this broken world, circumstances and people will hurt us, and sometimes, our choices hurt us. Still, I have learned that those who never come to understand and receive the gift of forgiveness fully will stay in sadness and darkness and are incapable of living in the fullness of God's love that He always intended for us.

It is a misconception that forgiveness and surrendering it to God are for the other person. Forgiveness does far more for the person choosing to forgive (whether for themselves or for others). It empowers them to be free from revenge, hate, and anger. Jesus gave us the gift of forgiveness, but we must open that gift! Once we open that gift, we actively run toward God by reading scripture, praying, serving others, and being generous with our time, resources, and gifts.

My experience has not been that a counselor or a support group is the answer, although I value both. Instead, I found my support in an intimate relationship with God. That is what our minds and hearts are seeking. And, it is available to each

## Forgiveness

and every one. All that is asked is that we receive Jesus in our hearts and begin to live a lifestyle of love. If you have never done that, repeat this prayer or one similar to begin the most important journey of your life.

> Prayer of Salvation:
>
> Heavenly Father, I come to You in the name of Jesus. I pray and ask Jesus to come into my heart and be Lord over my life. I confess that Jesus is Lord, and I believe in my heart that You raised Him from the dead. I ask for Your forgiveness as a sinner, and I let go of those events and people who have harmed me. I now trust and follow You as my Savior!

Live in the absolute truth that God loves you! Reading scripture daily is an open invitation to knowing who God is and His plans for you. But the Bible is a mighty book in size and meaning, so you might consider starting in the Gospels (Matthew, Mark, Luke, and John) to learn about Jesus' birth, ministry, death, and resurrection. Then, read the letters in the Bible (Romans, 1 Corinthians, Galatians, Ephesians, Philippians, and Colossians) to be reminded that we make the decisions to live by God's commands at the intersection of faith and life.

Or read the wisdom books (Psalms, Proverbs, Ecclesiastes, and Song of Songs) to know how to live loving God. Or read Genesis to understand the power and love of God to have put so much thought into creation. The Old and the New Testaments guide us on how to live. Get to know who God is, and join Jesus in His purpose to heal this world.

Pray daily. Both speak to God and listen to Him. God doesn't need your words to be perfect, but your heart must be honest. God invites you to step into His presence with prayer anywhere, anytime.

Engage in a community. Do not wait to be "perfect" (none of us will accomplish that on this side of heaven) before helping others. Great healing comes from thinking of others before yourself and fixing your eyes on Jesus!

Forgiveness of yourself or others is the most wonderful gift you could ever open, for it will lead to a stronger relationship with God through a lifestyle of scripture, prayer, and servanthood. God has always intended for us to live in the fullness of His love.

God is whispering to each of you reading this, the exact words He gave me to say to my daughter in the hospital, "You are safe now; I'm here; you are safe now." God put His Spirit in us when we welcomed Jesus into our hearts so we can sleep, wake, and walk confidently as we remain in God's competent and constant care.

> He will cover you with his feathers, and you will find refuge under his wings. (Psalm 91:4)

# 6

# Broken Promises

### SUSIE

All my life, I have felt that God has a place and a plan for my life. Through the eighth grade, I attended a parochial school and went through the motions of being a good, religious girl. I loved God, but I had no personal relationship with Him.

When I started high school, I drifted away from thoughts of God and started doing my own thing. At fifteen, I met a boy, and all my devotion became focused on him. We were always together through high school and college, and then we married and had a family. I was sure this was what God had planned for me all along, but I didn't draw Him into my life. I was too busy.

Still, God was tugging at me. We had new neighbors move in next door, and we met and developed a close relationship with them. He was a pastor, and they had moved into our town to start a new church.

As neighbors, we quickly became very close. They invited us to their church for the first anniversary service. We both truly enjoyed it, and eventually, my husband and I accepted Jesus Christ into our lives.

But like many people, we became even busier with life. We now had four biological children, whom I homeschooled. Over the years, we became foster parents to fifteen children and adopted two of them. During this time, my husband completed law school. Then, even though I had my degree as a teacher, I truly felt a need to get a nursing degree, too.

These were my plans, our plans for our life, but was God in those plans? I had the perfect life, or so I thought!

If you had asked me if I had a real and personal relationship with Jesus Christ, I would have said yes, absolutely. Unfortunately, I didn't know then what I know now.

In the summer of 2010, my relationship with my husband seemed to change. He grew cold and less caring, which had never been part of our relationship before. We had been together for thirty-eight years; he was my high school sweetheart. Then, the bottom of my world fell out!

In September, I found out he was having an affair with a woman from his work. In October, our youngest biological daughter was getting married. She wanted to wear my wedding dress, and I didn't want her to know what was going on yet, the agonizing heartbreak of watching her walk down the aisle in my wedding dress. No one knew what I was hiding behind my smiles that day.

November came, and I tried to get us to go to counseling. He went but remained cold and distant. I realized I was the only one trying. By December, he made it clear to me that he loved the other woman and would not give her up. So, I moved out.

I was devastated, to say the least. My plans and my perfect life were interrupted, and I emotionally spiraled into a pit of anxiety and depression. Few people knew how bad it had gotten for me. I couldn't eat or sleep, and I functioned on autopilot. My only refuge was listening to Christian music and praying.

I was living on my own, and I decided to start personal counseling. In the refuge of my music and prayer, God spoke to me! He reminded me that "Whoever dwells in the shelter of the Most-High will rest in the shadow of the Almighty. I will say of the Lord; He is my refuge and my fortress, my God, in whom I will trust" (Psalms 91:1–2). God was saying to me, "Just *trust me;* I still have a plan for your life." But, Lord, my life is such a mess. How can that be?! He said, "Let me show you what I see."

He revealed the image of the back of a tapestry, a tangled *mess* of strings with no sense to it. But turn it around, and you see a beautiful image. That is what He has for me! He sees the big picture, when all I see is the mess.

In a devotional by Chris Teigreen, he wrote, "If we will trust Him (the Lord) as our Refuge, we can know that we will never experience any catastrophe that is devoid of redemptive purpose. We will never see a trial or difficulty that is not under His sovereign, permissive hand that specifically ordains our steps and redeems our problems. He has a plan… Because we have been bought by God, nothing—not one single thing—can threaten our security within His plan."[1]

Truly, it is in our trials that we learn the most about God, and I am living proof of that!

In the book of Job, Job experiences a devasting loss, but he never turns his eyes away from God. Ultimately, he is given double what he lost because he clung to God and never let go through it all.

Another example of living for God in the midst of trials is Joseph, who was made doubly fruitful in the land of his affliction because he never lost sight of the God who was always with him.

When God's people lose what they were promised—whether through their own sin or someone else's—and continue to seek Him where He may be found, the result is always better than at first. God promises to all those in this world who will seek Him with all their heart: They will find Him, and in finding Him, they will be restored to what was. In clinging to the Lord, He promised us, "I will repay you for the years the locusts have eaten" (Joel 2:25).

It became apparent that my marriage was not going to be restored, and we eventually divorced, but my life has most certainly been restored. I clung to the promise that God would compensate for what had been taken away. I started my *slow* climb out of the anxiety and depression and chose to search for His plan for my life. It was still there! Was it easy? *No*! It has taken me twelve long years, but I am praising God daily.

As women, we often let our circumstances dictate the path we take. When it's hard, we frequently choose to go in another direction (the easier path, the one of least resistance). He promises to deliver us from our darkest moments. He will be, for us, a God of the impossible. Corrie Ten Boom says, "Faith sees the invisible, believes the unbelievable, and receives the impossible."[2]

Some days, climbing out of that hole seemed impossible, but I kept on believing that God is the God of new beginnings.

I got myself a new beginning tattoo: a Celtic symbol for "new beginning" and a second one with Jeremiah 29:11, which says, "For I know the plans I have for you, plans to prosper you and not to harm you, plans to give you hope and a future."³

I love what Priscilla Shirer says in her book *Life Interrupted*: "I don't want to let one more interruption send me off frantically dodging God's will and missing out on what He wants to accomplish in me and through me. I want my life to radiate what happens when God has a person's heart in His complete control, when every event or circumstance is simply another avenue to know Him better and show forth His glory."⁴ This interruption—whatever it is, no matter how big or small—represents your next best chance to see Him take center stage, to show you what He can do when the unexpected only makes you more expectant than ever.

I was ready for Him to take center stage in my life—something I honestly had not done before all of these distractions: my husband, children, church, and friends. Then, the Lord brought another interruption into my life, as He sometimes does to test our integrity and commitment. I lost my job. But *this* time, I saw the interruption for what it was: part of His divine plan.

He is *so* good! I started seeing how He had this plan for me all along: nursing school (while I was still married), two jobs, and two condos up north, available to me at different times. Oh, how He has provided for me.

His plan for me was never interrupted; I was the one who put it on pause, but it was a pause of immense growth. *A true, real, and personal relationship with Jesus Christ* as my best friend. God promised to fill the vacant places in my life. *No one* else can do that. Not a husband, children, friends, or church. Jeremiah 29:11: "For I know the plans I have for you," declares the LORD, "plans to prosper you and not harm you, plans to give you hope and a future."⁵

Reaching *beyond* the Pain

I have to admit I wanted to erase that part of *my history*, but our past is part of God's story. In her Esther study, Beth Moore says, "You cannot amputate your history from your destiny; you cannot become the person He means you to be without it. Esther's history was that she was Jewish, which ultimately became her destiny: to save the Jewish people of the kingdom. That, my friends, is *redemption*!" As Beth continues, "Your past and your future share the same root, the root of *Jesus Christ*. He is the pause between the past and the future."

To paraphrase Mordecai's words to Esther in Esther 4:14, "Perhaps this is the moment for which you have been created."[6]

---

[1] Chris Teigreen, *The One Year Worship the King Devotional: 365 Daily Bible Readings to Inspire Praise*, Walk Thru the Bible, Tyndale House Publisher, Inc., 2008

[2] Corrie Ten Boom, *Jesus is Victor*, Fleming H. Rebell, Co. Ada, Michigan, 1985

[3] NIV

[4] Priscilla Shirer, *Life Interrupted*. Pg. 13, P & B Publishing Group, Nashville, Tennessee, 2011

[5] NIV

[6] NIV

# 7

# Second Chances

## JULIE

While attending a chapel service during college, I felt a deep calling to serve God and follow His purpose for my life. Though I didn't know exactly what that would look like, I knew I couldn't ignore it. After graduating, I went on staff with Young Life, an organization dedicated to introducing high school students to Jesus and helping them grow in their faith. I dove into the ministry wholeheartedly. I loved working with teens, loved Jesus, and felt truly privileged to serve in that capacity.

Through this ministry, I met my future husband, Bill. He had just returned from mission work in Costa Rica and was volunteering with Young Life. We quickly bonded over shared interests and dreams. Together, we led a group of kids to summer camp and worked alongside each other for a year and a half. When he proposed, I didn't hesitate—I eagerly looked forward to our life together.

Soon after our wedding, we accepted a mission opportunity in the Abacos, a series of small islands in the Bahamas.

## Reaching *beyond* the Pain

We were excited about the adventure ahead—serving at a school and a church in this tropical paradise. Little did I know that it was here that my faith would be tested in ways I never expected, and I would be challenged to trust the Lord like never before.

It unfolded gradually; honestly, I can't remember all the details. Perhaps that's God's protection, sparing me from the full weight of the memories. Small lies and subtle inconsistencies began to surface with Bill—nothing major at first, but enough to make me question my own sanity. I tried to make sense of it all, desperately searching for answers. It wasn't until nearly a year later that the puzzle pieces started to come together, and what I uncovered was heartbreaking. Bill had been having an affair and was facing legal trouble for embezzling money. A deep chasm had formed between us, and I no longer recognized the man I had married. This felt impossible to overcome, and I felt utterly hopeless.

We left the islands abruptly. I returned home a shell of the person I had been—empty, joyless, just going through the motions. I wrestled with many questions for God, wondering how He could allow this to happen when I earnestly sought Him. But even in my brokenness, God surrounded me with amazing people who spoke truth into my life and loved me through the pain. I knew I had reached a crossroads in my faith. Would I cling to the truths I had shared with my Young Life kids? Could God *really* heal me, make something beautiful out of my brokenness? Could I trust Him after such a profound disappointment?

It didn't happen overnight, but slowly, through the steady foundation of God's Word, I was strengthened and healed by His grace. My marriage was still in tatters, but I held fast to

God and His promises, even when it felt like everything else was falling apart.

Over the next few years, I continued to pray for my marriage. At that time, God brought me to 2 Chronicles 20:17: "You will not have to fight this battle. Take up your positions; stand firm and see the deliverance the Lord will give you... Do not be afraid; do not be discouraged. Go out to face them tomorrow, and the Lord will be with you."

Looking back, I can see how God fought for me, gently guiding me through the process of healing and ultimately releasing me from my marriage. In the end, Bill continued his affairs and engaged in illegal practices, and God made it clear He was releasing me from the covenant I had made. I knew, without a doubt, that He had freed me.

I was an endurance runner. From my early teens, running long distances was part of my life. I ran in college and continued to race in over thirty marathons and ultramarathons after graduation. It wasn't unusual for female athletes, particularly runners, to experience irregular menstrual or absent cycles due to low body fat and intense physical activity. I assumed my cycle would eventually normalize once I reduced my training intensity. But after years of no change, I decided to take action and ask my doctor to test for polycystic ovary syndrome (PCOS) specifically. This hormonal condition affects women of reproductive age and is the leading cause of infertility. My doctor was initially skeptical, as I seemed like an atypical patient.

The turning point came after I had just completed the Boston Marathon. I had missed two phone calls—one from my brother and the other from my doctor. Still riding the post-race high, I didn't immediately return the calls. When I finally listened to the messages, my brother informed me that while I was out of state, he had run into Bill, still my husband at the time, with another woman. I don't remember all the details he shared, but I knew, deep in my heart, that this was the final blow to my marriage. It felt as though everything had come crashing down.

I took a day to process what I had just learned before calling my doctor back. Less than twenty-four hours later, I received the second blow: The test results confirmed my suspicion—I had PCOS.

When I made the decision to stay in my marriage and seek God's redemption, I had also made the difficult choice not to have children. I didn't want to bring kids into the complexity and uncertainty of my situation. While I believed that God could restore my marriage and transform Bill's heart, I also knew I couldn't complicate things further until He had done His work in both of us.

I watched longingly as my friends and family had babies. It was the natural progression in life—getting married and having babies. I had always dreamed of having children. I imagined a large family gathering around a dinner table, filled with laughter and clattering dishes. My parents had created a loving, nurturing home for me and my siblings, and I had always envisioned the same for myself. To consider that children might not be a part of my story was a tough pill to swallow.

These two profound disappointments—losing my marriage and confronting infertility—left me reeling, grappling with questions for God I didn't know how to answer.

I can still remember my college prayer: "Lord, make my life count for Your Kingdom. Pour my life out as a sacrifice for Your purposes."

A friend once shared something that stuck with me: "God doesn't use people who haven't weathered the storms. He uses those who've been tested, who come out the other side faithful and refined. There is a cost to having a platform and purpose."

I can't say the journey has been easy. Even now, there are moments when my heart still aches unexpectedly for the family I've longed for. At times, the void feels so deep and raw that I whisper, *"Why, Lord, is this my story?"* But in those moments, I'm reminded that we all face a choice: to trust that God is the master architect of a story we can't fully see or to choose disappointment, to linger there long enough for bitterness to take root and steal away our joy.

I've learned that embracing God's plan—even when it doesn't make sense in the world's eyes—brings a kind of joy that is unshaken by circumstances. It's a joy born of trust, a testimony of faith in the One who is faithful, even when our hearts don't yet understand.

When Bill and I parted ways, I was thirty years old. During the turbulent four years of our marriage, I grieved not only the loss of my relationship but also the dream of having a family. I walked through some very dark seasons, but even in those painful moments, God protected my heart from bitterness. He restored my joy and planted seeds of hope in the midst of my suffering. Over time, He gently began to open my heart to the possibility of loving again.

At thirty-three, I was reintroduced to Jason, a family friend's son who had also gone through a divorce. What started as a friendship gradually evolved into something deeper. Jason was the father of three young girls. The first time I met his girls, he invited me to breakfast, and as we finished and walked out of the restaurant, one of the girls slipped her hand into mine and held it tightly as we walked down the sidewalk. A flood of emotions overwhelmed me. *"Is this what it feels like to be part of a family... to have kids?"* I fought back tears as my heart experienced something it hadn't before.

As Jason and I navigated the complexities of a long-distance relationship, we were both aware of the challenges ahead, especially what it might look like to blend our lives and families. We weren't naive, but we were hopeful.

When Jason and I married, I became a stepmom. I wasn't sure what to expect, but I knew it would require a lot of work. What I didn't anticipate was the deep love that would grow in my heart for these three girls. No, they weren't biologically mine, and they had a mother who loves them dearly. But I got to play a special role in their lives. Over the years, I prayed for them, cheered them on, encouraged them, and had the privilege of sharing Jesus with them.

By the time Jason and I married, my chances of pregnancy had significantly diminished. With PCOS, there are ways to support fertility, but after 35, it becomes increasingly difficult. On top of that, I had labral tears in both hips, requiring invasive procedures. It became clear that I wouldn't have biological children of my own.

There are still waves of sorrow—days when I question God's reasons for this chapter of my story. But I don't stay there. Instead, I choose to thank God for the opportunity to love three incredible girls that He placed in my life with a specific purpose. I think back to my days as a Young Life leader, when so many girls came through my life. We'd pray together on my living room floor, laugh at football games, and study the Bible, learning about Jesus. God was preparing me for one of the most important missions of my life: to love and invest in these three young ladies, helping them grow in their faith and understanding of the Lord.

My purpose came with a cost, but I'm deeply grateful for the role I get to play. I consider it a high calling. Though my life looks different than what I would have chosen, I chose to trust the Lord, and I chose to allow His joy to permeate my life. After all, He is writing my story, and I know He is good.

I'll leave you with the verses that comfort me:

> Therefore, we do not lose heart. Though outwardly we are wasting away, yet inwardly we are being renewed day by day. For our light and momentary troubles are achieving for us an eternal glory that far outweighs them all. So, we fix our eyes not on what is seen, but on what is unseen, since what is seen is temporary, but what is unseen is eternal. (2 Corinthians 4:16–18)

> When you pass through the waters, I will be with you; and when you pass through the rivers, they will not sweep over you. When you walk through the fire, you will not be burned; the flames will not set you ablaze. (Isaiah 43:2)

> Consider it pure joy, my brothers and sisters, whenever you face trials of many kinds, because you know that the testing of your faith produces perseverance. Let perseverance finish its work so that you may be mature and complete, not lacking anything. (James 1:2–4)

> I have told you these things, so that in me you may have peace. In this world you will have trouble. But take heart! I have overcome the world. (John 16:33)

# 8

# Set Free

### KIPP

When I meet or work with various people, I often ask if I may tell them my story. I do that with the hope that my story may move them to live a better life, so let me tell you my story. I went from an addictive love of drugs and alcohol to a love of my Lord and Savior—and a love for those around me. I damaged and ruined lives along the way, and I went a long way toward ruining my life as well. Only through a dramatic encounter with God did my life change for the better.

My bad habits began so simply and easily when I was in the eighth grade. During the Christmas break, I went to my neighbor's house, and we went down into the basement, where his parents had a bar. Foolishly wanting to try it out, we began testing the whiskey and ended up really chugging it down. I became intoxicated and even got sick from drinking so much. It came time for me to go home and eat dinner, and somehow, I managed to hide my drunken condition from my parents, whom I loved very much. I was changed, though. The feeling that came from drinking became the most enjoyable and essential thing in my life. On the weekends, I started seeking alcohol, and soon I decided to try marijuana, which quickly became a part of my daily life. Peer pressure began to influence my life, too. A lot of the kids in the neighborhood smoked cigarettes and drank. Previously, I could say "no" because I enjoyed my sports so much, but I finally gave in to it. It is sad to realize how quickly alcohol and drugs took over my life.

That simple beginning in the eighth grade started me on a downward path that lasted for years. I continued to play football, basketball, and baseball in the ninth grade while also passing all my schoolwork, but in the tenth grade, I didn't play any sports and only passed three of my classes. By then, I had used marijuana every day and indulged in the occasional speed, acid, and, finally, cocaine. I hung out with older guys, and we typically shared the stuff. If I had a few dollars here and there, I would buy. Of course, I needed more money to supply my habit, so I worked a few weekends for my neighbors who owned a carpet-cleaning business, often skipping school in the eleventh and twelfth grades to work more with one of the carpet-cleaning crews. I didn't graduate and continued working for them and similar companies until I was about twenty-eight.

During that time, I was rather callous toward those around me. I took everything for granted, especially people. I didn't recognize them as having any value, and I never showed them any compassion. My sole focus was on what I wanted, which was predominantly drugs and alcohol.

When I was twenty-two, I began a relationship with a woman, and within a year, our first daughter was born. We never married but remained together for seven years, and eventually, we welcomed a second daughter into our home. I was still smoking pot daily, and then crack became available. It was just so easy to get. As you can imagine, our family life was not good, and our relationship continued to deteriorate, though we always took good care of the children. We worked different shifts, which helped care for the children, but my mom also helped.

Eventually, we settled into a pattern of going our own ways on the weekends, and things got progressively worse and worse. Our daughters were six and three years old when we finally split up.

I had begun living with my parents when someone from an adoption agency came to see me, informing me that another woman with whom I had gotten pregnant was putting the baby up for adoption. The adoption agency asked for my information in case the baby ever wanted to contact me when she was grown. Years later, we had contact, brought about by my second daughter having a DNA test, which revealed that she had another sister. I was able to talk with my "new" daughter, but it was during the COVID crisis, and she did not want to get together. However, we have communicated online. She is a Facebook friend, and that is where I must leave it.

The next fifteen years of my life were a mixture of trying to do better and failing miserably. Not long after the break-up of the seven-year relationship, I met my wife, Lisa, and we've been together for thirty years. When we met, she had three kids, and I had two daughters. Unfortunately, I continued to be a weekend dad.

When we met, Lisa was living with her mom, and we moved in together right away. I was twenty-eight then, and that is also when I left the floor care business and shifted to the drywall trade. I worked hourly for three years with several companies and started a drywall hanging business, which was very good for a time. Now I'm a union carpenter, still doing drywall.

Unfortunately, my drug use continued to increase. I didn't use cocaine every day, but it happened spasmodically, sometimes once a month, sometimes less. When I went out, I would often be gone for days, and Lisa would usually throw me out. Then, I would try to seek help and would improve for a time, going to rehab or attending meetings such as Alcoholics Anonymous or Narcotics Anonymous. Sometimes, I stayed at my mom's or my brothers or whoever would let me stay. I was in a cycle of seeking help and making some progress but then going back to my unhealthy habits.

I have always said that my story was part of the crack and opioid epidemics. Opioids became popular, and it was during the last eight years of my drug use that I had opioids every day. You must have it every day, or you can't function, and I experienced that for pretty much the whole eight years. The majority of the stuff that I purchased on the street was heroin. Alcohol was still a minor factor, but I was mainly seeking opiates, whether it was heroin, OxyContin, Vicodin, or Morphine. I would use whatever I could get my hands on that was an opiate-based drug, which was easier to hide. This was the darkest time. I was using whatever I could afford. If I had a lot, I'd take a lot. It seemed like the more I got, the quicker it would be gone, and I would be seeking more. I was so sick and tired of it, but the drugs dominated my life.

Because of those drug binges, Lisa had to throw me out of the house at least twenty to thirty times. The pattern was for me to beg and ask, "Please let me come back home." Usually, within a couple of weeks to a month, she'd let me return, and we would go back to our everyday lifestyle. Because of the children in the home, I did try to limit how much my addictive behavior was evident. I was going to work every day, and if I had my opiates, it would be pretty much a "normal" life.

The AA book says something to the effect that "their alcoholic life becomes their only normal life." When I had my opiates, I felt normal, but without them, I always felt sick. If I had them, I believe a tornado could go through the house, and it wouldn't have even phased me. I laughed with the kids and had fun with them. However, when I didn't have my opiates, it wasn't good because that's all I could think about. All my focus was on how I could get more. My temper would also be short. I didn't care about anybody or anything else, and my needs always came first. In retrospect, I feel terrible because even if my kids or our family needed something, the drugs were my first priority, and paying the bills was a distant second. We lived that way for years and years. To my shame, my wife and family suffered greatly.

During all those years of darkness, I did occasionally seek help through AA or NA treatments. I have even been to outpatient treatments, some initiated by two drunk-driving convictions that mandated such treatment. The longest I ever stayed sober on my own was nine months—nine months of complete sobriety—but it did not last.

Now, we get to the good part of my story, the part that I love to tell. It was fifteen years ago that I went on another crack binge while still using opiates every day. Understandably, my wife threw me out of the house again. I was staying at my mom's, and Lisa's cousin called me to say that she was trying to get sober from alcohol. She told me she had found an excellent meeting and suggested I check it out with her.

I was reluctant at first, as this is my wife's cousin. Eventually, she got me to this meeting, which was called "the grateful group." Again, as I did at many other meetings, they let me talk. I broke down and told my story. I was just broken, completely broken. It was no more than what I had said at other times, but something was different this time. At this meeting, the guy chairing the meeting gave me the book *Alcoholics Anonymous*. He said, "I want you to pick a sponsor right now." I had always heard that you should get to know someone before asking them to sponsor you, but this chairperson said, "No, these men want to help you fix this, so pick a sponsor right now." When I looked around, I picked a man named Tim, who's been sober for some time. Looking back, I can see how God was at work in that whole situation. At that time, I had no car or anything else, for that matter. Tim lived only a block from my mom's house, where I was staying, and he gave me a ride. Stopping in front of the house, he asked, "Can I pray with you?" That was something that no one had ever said to me before. He took my hands and said a prayer. I remember how weird it seemed, but I just went along with it.

I kept going to the meetings, and it was different in that they opened the book *Alcoholics Anonymous* at every meeting, reading aloud from the book and then talking about it. That was certainly the right way to touch my heart, for it pointed me to God (though AA leaves the idea of God open to each person's understanding). It was the first book I ever really read. It captivated me and truly got me excited about sobriety.

That book, which is Scripture-inspired all the way, is still part of my life. I love one of the sentences in the book: "Either God is everything, or he's nothing." It truly opened my eyes.

In hindsight, when change fully and finally came, it happened quickly, and I can truthfully say that I cannot claim to be the one who reached out to the Lord, but that He reached out to me.

I had been faithfully going to the group meetings and continuing to read the book. A chapter called "We Agnostics" suggests that deep down inside each and every one of us is the fundamental idea of God. When I read that, my arms started tingling, and I felt this peace come over me like I had never felt before. I felt almost as if I was elevated. It seemed like I was almost floating; I was so peaceful. At that moment, my mom, dad, brothers and sisters, wife, and kids started running through my head. The word "blessed" kept coming to me, just the word "blessed." That word was not part of my normal vocabulary; it was just not a part of my brain. I didn't know where the feelings and the ideas had come from, though I knew it must be from God. At that moment, I sensed that if that was happening, I was free. Surprisingly, I started crying and laughing uncontrollably for about fifteen or twenty minutes.

I was sitting on my mom's couch in her living room. She was in her room, and I remember that I kept watching and wondering if she was going to think I was losing my mind because I was crying uncontrollably and laughing at the same time. I can't explain it, but I felt assured I had really experienced this and that it was true. Since that fifteen-to-twenty-minute experience, I've never touched another drug or drop of alcohol.

Something about reading the paragraph containing the sentence, "God is everything, or He's nothing at all," touched my heart and opened me wide open.

That incredible experience was a beautiful gift from God that truly changed me in so many ways, so my story does not end there. Growing up, neither my family nor Lisa's was God-centered at all. As a kid, I remember my mom wanting us to go to church, but we never engaged in worship, prayer, or

Bible reading. The same was true in my wife's family, but God changed me and continues to change us, even now.

After that experience at my mom's, I increasingly desired to read the Bible, and in those early days, I would wake up in the morning sobbing, not because of pain but because I was filled with joy. I was overwhelmed with the Holy Spirit and was filled with so much gratitude that I would weep for joy. I started going to church, and after about a year, I was baptized. When I wrote my testimony for baptism, I remember being so overwhelmed with joy that I cried the whole time. I kept going to my AA meetings and doing anything I could to soak up more time with the Lord, including attending small groups and an early Sunday morning church service. That worship service featured a more traditional style of church music, but then, about eight years ago, I was introduced to some contemporary Christian music and was really impacted. That was my style of music, so when I found that music on the radio, it brought me to tears. Now, Lisa and I regularly attend Unity Fest and other Christian concerts. We really enjoy worshipping.

Though my life was truly changed, I suspect that my rapid transition was somewhat unsettling to those close to me. I don't fully understand how it affected Lisa, but I suspect some of my family felt as if I was trying to push God on them. Therefore, since surrendering to God fifteen years ago, I've been trying not to be too radical at home and allow others to embrace Him at their own pace. I have been blessed to communicate regularly with my first two daughters, and though they both live out of state, they come to visit from time to time. I also went down to Texas to see my oldest daughter when her son was born. I look for opportunities to tell our grown children about the Lord and the incredible work that He has done in my life. They listen, and I trust that they will eventually respond.

Lisa and I have grown older together, so we don't have as much energy as we used to have. Often, we simply want to go home for dinner and relax in front of the TV. Like most folks, there are occasional disagreements, but they are not the fights we used to have. Of course, there are still bills to pay, which can be challenging. Life is life, and I'm enjoying it.

I love life; I love people. I still work as a union carpenter, and sometimes the job ends, and there doesn't seem to be another job for me. I could always be laid off, but we have faith, and I believe God probably has something better for me. Somehow, it always works out, and He opens employment doors for me. New job sites are a blessing, giving me a chance to tell of God's glory and power to more people in the construction trade. Over the years, I've gladly told my story to many of those guys. I tell them that fifteen years ago, I wasn't like I am now, and I share how I was set free.

For me, it has been incredible to connect what Jesus did on the cross for me and what happened to me that night fifteen years ago. I am convinced that God the Father touched me and that through His Holy Spirit, I experienced healing that nothing else could provide. Alcoholics Anonymous describes addiction as being rather like having an allergy. Not everyone has that allergy, but some people take in a substance only once and develop a craving, which they call the phenomenon of craving. Not everybody has that, but it doesn't go away for those who do. My craving remains, and I believe I'll always be a recovered addict, but when the Holy Spirit entered my life, He set me free from the power of cravings and addiction, just as Jesus' death on the cross set me free from the power of sin and death. I have been fully and gloriously set free.

I like to say that I've been restored to sanity when it comes to alcohol and drugs, and in God's strength, I will never put something in me that I know will be harmful. I feel like a switch went off the moment I surrendered to Him, and I have not touched another drug or drop of alcohol. I know with all my heart that it isn't anything I've done. I didn't do this; God did it. It was all God, and I continue to praise Him and seek Him constantly. It's that simple.

# 9

# Shattered Dreams

## LAQUITA

Who would ever have guessed that the phone call would drastically change our lives? It was from a supervisor at the restaurant where our daughter, Cynthia, worked while finishing her last semester in college. The woman at the end of the line abruptly informed me, "Your daughter has Huntington's Disease."

I indignantly replied, "No, she does not. We know that she is at risk for that disease, but she does not have it." As we continued talking, though, my certainty was shattered as the woman convinced me that she had some knowledge of neurological diseases. I tearfully realized that we must check it out, so we made an appointment with a neurologist at the University of Michigan Hospital in Ann Arbor.

When we applied for a second adoption twenty-five years earlier, we already had a beautiful little girl, so we offered to take a handicapped child, as we knew that often those children were never placed for adoption. Cynthia's "handicap" was that her grandmother had Huntington's Disease, giving her a chance of getting that progressive genetic disease that had no cure. We had never heard of HD, and the little research we could find was not in the least encouraging, as it talked about possible psychiatric and behavioral problems. That really put me off, but though I was reluctant, we both felt that we should continue praying about it. The Lord soon made it clear to us that He wanted us to adopt that precious little girl, and she was brought to live with us when she was eight and a half months of age. She was a healthy child who progressed normally, though with difficulty during her teen years. The specter of HD was almost forgotten—until that phone call from the restaurant supervisor.

At that time, there was no test for HD, so several visits to the University of Michigan Hospital were required before the neurologist determined through observation and family history that, indeed, Cynthia had that dreaded disease. We had never met anyone with HD, so we did not know what to expect. We had a lot to learn.

It was a hard time, made more difficult by a history of conflict with Cynthia. Our struggle with her started with her puberty. She became belligerent and defiant and was generally very hard to live with. We thought she was just being a very difficult teenager, but looking back, we believe that HD was already at work in her brain, contributing to her challenging behavior. Research now shows that aberrant behavior can begin years before physical symptoms are manifested. But during her teen and early adult years, we had no idea that her actions could be the result of HD.

Though Cynthia was very trying as a teenager, I now realize that a lot of the conflict was my fault. Of course, I did not fully see that at the time, but I now believe that I was trying to get her to conform to what I thought she ought to be. She and

I were very different in personality, and I was not appreciating her free spirit that was so unlike my own. I resented the trouble she was bringing into the household; in fact, I was having a real pity party. I had never dealt with someone who was so ungrateful and unlovable. Undoubtedly, I had a lot to learn about what love really means.

It was a great relief when we delivered Cynthia to her dorm room in an Ohio college, but there were still problems. She made friends, but they were all the partying type. Cynthia had been a top student, but her grades began to plummet. After frequent failing of classes, we finally told her that we would no longer support her financially. As a compromise, she asked if she could attend the Christian college in Texas that Elton and I had attended, and we agreed to support her there. In the middle of her second semester in Texas, she disappeared without telling anyone where she had gone. We were quite certain that she had returned to her college in Ohio, and after a week, she did contact us. She settled down somewhat and got a waitressing job in a nice restaurant, and it was then that I received the phone call from her supervisor that resulted in her eventual diagnosis of Huntington's Disease.

Cynthia finally managed to graduate from college with a degree in geriatrics, and she asked if we would support her in the town where she had done her internship, which was also where her boyfriend lived. We helped her find a nice apartment, but by the end of the summer, it was clear that she was unable to cope with the ordinary demands of life. We finally brought her home to live with us, and she soon announced that she was pregnant. We, who had always tried to teach our children to live lives of purity before God, were devastated at the news. Making it somewhat more understandable, though, was that we had learned that commonly, some persons with HD manifest hypersexuality and in general show poor judgment and little or no impulse control.

We urged Cynthia to let the baby be adopted out, but she adamantly refused. It became obvious that we would be caring for the baby since Cynthia could not even care for herself, so we asked if we could adopt the baby. Cynthia readily and eagerly assented. Elton and I had enjoyed our few "empty-nest" years, but rather suddenly, we were caregivers of Cynthia and about to be parents of an infant again. Our lives were drastically changed. I was happily teaching university courses, and though I tried to continue teaching after little Rachel was born, it soon became obvious that I needed to be at home.

Cynthia liked the idea of being a mother, and occasionally, she would give the baby a bottle, but mostly, she refused to do any of the infant care, especially the messy and difficult parts. The baby was a blessing and a joy to us, but our relationship with Cynthia was another matter. We often had to refuse Cynthia's permission to do something dangerous for the baby, such as when we discovered her crossing in the middle of a very busy street with the baby in her pram. Of course, such episodes led to a major battle.

Cynthia began shoplifting cigarettes, and we ended up in court with her more than once. We finally left her in jail one night, hoping that would teach her not to shoplift. Conflicts continued. One Sunday afternoon, she was angry with us, and we decided to take a walk to give her time to calm down, but instead, she followed us around the neighborhood, yelling at us. We then took the baby and left for an evening church service, returning home to find Cynthia lying across her bed and unresponsive. That suicide gesture landed her in a local hospital and then in the psychiatric ward of the U of M hospital in

Ann Arbor. After great difficulty, Cynthia was finally placed into an adult foster care home in Detroit.

Having Cynthia out of the home was a tremendous relief, but I also felt very guilty, knowing that some conflicts were largely my fault. I had all too often found myself angry and resentful. I knew I had failed Cynthia because I was not sympathetic to her plight. She was facing a terrible and progressive disease that would gradually take away all her ability to walk, speak, and eat. Why couldn't I be more loving and understanding? I prayed often, asking for forgiveness. I felt like I was in the middle of a dangerous stormy sea and about to go down. I couldn't escape the storm, but I was holding on to the Lord's lifeline as hard as possible. That was all that kept me up.

My struggle was not one I could share very easily. When I did try to share with others, I could often see that my friend did not understand my dilemma, so I just mostly quit trying. I had one friend in Texas who came to stay with us for a week, which was a blessing. One day in church, I felt the Lord telling me to share with a certain friend, so I asked to go see her at her house. She has gone to heaven now, but I still remember with gratitude talking to her and crying on her shoulder.

My principal help, though, came from the Lord. I read Scripture regularly, and I often prayed on my knees with Cynthia in a care home. I often asked for forgiveness and asked for His help. One incident especially stands out in my mind. I was at church listening to a missionary who had been in South Africa, and he was talking about the great need for forgiveness concerning the racial situation in that country. While he was talking, the Lord spoke to me, telling me that I needed to forgive Cynthia. I had never realized that I needed to forgive her. On the contrary, I thought she needed to ask *our* forgiveness! I went through the process of forgiving Cynthia, and it freed me to be loving and compassionate toward her—and to have the joy of the Lord in my heart.

In talking to the Lord and asking for forgiveness after Cynthia was placed in care, I often added that I wished that I could do it all over again—I was sure that I would do a better job a second time. Well, the joke was on me, as the Lord granted my wish! About a year after Cynthia died at age forty-two, Rachel, who was almost sixteen by then, began showing physical signs of Huntington's Disease. We watched carefully, and it became obvious to us that she, too, had the gene. A test for the HD gene had been developed, and doctors were finally persuaded that her symptoms justified her being tested. Just before she was eighteen, Rachel was diagnosed with HD. It was a terrible blow to her, shattering her dreams. She knew what was ahead for her, as she had watched Cynthia's decline and her debilitation at the end.

Rachel went into a deep depression, and her behavior was just as difficult as Cynthia's had been. Like her birth mother, Rachel was in and out of psychiatric wards. Rachel, too, became pregnant, but this time, we were in our mid-70s, so the Lord provided by putting it in the hearts of Christian friends to adopt the baby. We knew them well; in fact, the adoptive mother had been one of Rachel's youth workers. We were so thankful for the Lord's provision for that precious little boy.

Months before Rachel was officially diagnosed, I began preparing for what was coming by memorizing verses regarding trust in the Lord in the middle of fear and trouble. And, of course, we prayed a lot. The Lord gave us a verse on the morning of Cynthia's funeral: "In everything give thanks" (1 Thessalonians 5:18), and we have tried to practice that command faithfully. And we are doing it differently. We have learned to pray immediately when confronted with another problem. We have learned to show our love to Rachel even when she is unlovable. We have learned to trust the Lord in all things. No, we haven't reached perfection, but we have come a long way with the Lord's help.

When we said "yes" to the Lord's telling us to adopt Cynthia all those years ago, we had no idea how hard—nor how long—the journey would be. We are still in the midst of that journey with HD, as Rachel is now thirty and in the latter stages of the disease. It has not been easy, but we are thankful for the privilege of doing a hard job for the Lord. We know that we are better people for having gone through the fray. We give our Lord all the praise.

For caregivers of patients with Huntington's Disease, the national association, the Huntington's Disease Society of America, is based in New York. Their contact information:

> Helpline: 800-345-HDSA (4372)
> National Office: 212-242-1968
> Email: HDSAinfo@HDSA.org
> or the link: https/hdsa.org

They can give information about support groups in your area. If you live in Jackson, MI, the nearest support group is in Adrian, MI. Their contact information:

> 517-260-7886
> bilsprow@comcast.net

Laquita Higgs and Elton Higgs have written a book called *Shattered Dreams—But Hope*. This is an excellent book for people who may be caregivers. I encourage anyone to order this book from Amazon! Several people who have read the book have also found it helpful to other caregivers.

# 10

# Walking in Faith

**BILL**

Diana asked me to tell my story, but where do I start? Well, as they all say, "The best place to start is at the beginning." So, here goes.

Hi, my name is Bill Bradshaw, born on July 11, 1959, and—

"No, no, no."

"What's wrong, Diana... Oh, not *that* far back? Just the recent story of my double amputation, how it impacted my life, and the role that my faith had in maintaining joy throughout it all? Okay, let me start again."

Everything began at the start of 2023 when a blister developed on the big toe of my right foot. "No big deal," I thought. I called my podiatrist and set an appointment for shortly thereafter.

The doctor said, "Well, we will keep an eye on it," which I later learned meant doing nothing but just that. Week after week, month after month, I went back for her to look at it. During this time, the blister had turned into a black spot, and over time, the entire toe turned black and began to decay. The last time I went back to see the doctor, she took about two steps into the room and told my wife to get me to the emergency room, so we went to the University of Michigan Emergency Room.

Once we arrived at U of M, I was given antibiotics via IV immediately, and within a few days, they determined that I needed to have the toe amputated. A few days after the procedure, I was released. I booked a follow-up appointment with the surgeon for a later date, and it was at that appointment that I was told not only was gangrene found in the tissue but in the bone as well. By this point, my foot was starting to turn black. The doctor said that because the gangrene was spreading so quickly, the only way to stop the progression of the gangrene would be to perform a below-the-knee amputation (referred to as a BKA).

At that moment, I took about two minutes to feel sorry for myself and shed a few tears. Then, I turned to my Savior and Lord Jesus Christ to tell Him that this time and through this trial, I would not turn my back on Him and walk away as I had before (a story for another time; I digress). Then, in turn, I told Satan that he could throw whatever trial at me he may, but I'm not going to walk away from Jesus.

Then came the day: June 27, 2023. With my wife Cindy by my side, we took on this trial together. She was there for the surgery, the recovery, and the rehabilitation. She was there every day that I was in the hospital. Not only physically but also spiritually. I felt her prayers before, during, and after. She helped me fully accept God's will for me. I felt God's peace, which was beyond my understanding, and I know that God is always with me. My wife is truly my strength and support in all ways.

## Walking in Faith

There was a time during my recovery when I felt Jesus speaking to me. I was lying in my hospital bed and reading John 11:35, which reads, "Jesus wept." Immediately after I read that, I heard Jesus say, "And I wept over you, too." When I heard His voice, I started crying and could not stop. I realized that the Lord of the universe loves me and cares about what happens to me. I drew close to Him, and He to me. That's how this trial has changed my life because, with faith, all things are possible.

After a week or so, I was transferred to a rehabilitation facility to learn how to live with one leg until I could be fitted with a prosthetic leg. While in rehab, nurses, therapists, and fellow patients often asked me, "Why are you always so happy?" That gave me the opportunity to share my faith and belief in Jesus. Also, in situations like this, you can either laugh or cry. Something I know about myself is that I love to laugh; I believe that Jesus is living through me and allowing others to see Jesus working in me. This is what makes it all worth it: when God uses you for His purpose.

So, toward the end of July, I was finally back home and waiting to heal in order to go through the process of being fitted for a prosthetic. On December 20, 2023, I received my new leg and was ready to learn how to walk again. I set up a rehabilitation appointment for January 8, 2024.

That's the end, right? Well, think again. In January of 2024, I was taking a shower and preparing for church. While doing so, I looked at my left foot and noticed it was beet red. I called for my wife to look at it, and as soon as she did, she said we were going straight back to the Emergency Room. Once we got to U of M Emergency, I was assigned a room and started IVs yet again. This time, though, after some time and testing, the doctor told me there was nothing they could do for me.

Normally, in situations like this, they would amputate the toe, but due to a lack of blood flow, they could not do this because it would not heal. So, the doctor performed an angioplasty and placed a stent in the artery to increase blood flow. That procedure seemed to do the trick. The doctor decided to do the toe amputation, and I was back home after a few days.

But by now, we know it's not that simple.

After about two months, we returned to the doctor for a follow-up appointment. We were told that due to the extremely slow healing of the toe amputation site and the fourth and fifth toes now showing signs of infection as well, he needed to perform a procedure called a transmetatarsal amputation. In simpler terms, this is the removal of the entire toe at the end of the foot. Afterward, it appeared everything was going well. But, after about three months, we returned for yet another appointment, and the doctor told us that the foot was not going to heal from this last surgery. The only option left was another below-the-knee amputation. Of course, that news was a shock, especially since the previous appointment had felt so positive. However, because I knew that Jesus was with me before, I knew that He would be with me this time as well. And so, on April 16, 2024, the below-the-knee amputation of the left leg was completed. Everything went just as well as the right leg. By the way, I should take the time to mention that for both surgeries, I had no pain—thanks be to God for this and so many other blessings as well.

During this recovery, I experienced something that I call a "God sighting." Once again, I was lying in bed reading my Bible; the surgeon came into my room to check in on me. Before asking how I was doing, he saw me reading and asked me, "What book are you reading?"

I told him, "The book of Acts."

## Walking in Faith

He said, "So am I! What chapter are you in?"

I responded, "Chapter 4." He told me he was in Chapter 6. After that, he proceeded with the normal doctor stuff.

"How are you feeling?" Then, he looked at the surgical site. But the big takeaway from this was the realization that my surgeon is a Christian; so all this time, through all of the procedures and surgeries, he allowed God to use him as well. It just goes to show that God is in all things and that with faith, all things are possible.

Again, after a few weeks, I was released from the hospital. But this time, I was able to go straight home. After about three months of healing, I started the process of getting another prosthetic leg. By September 2024, the leg was ready to be picked up. Then, in October 2024, the final appointment with the surgeon came, and he gave me the all-clear once and for all. I was fully healed, and no further procedures were needed.

As my story comes to an end, how do I wrap it all up? Simply by saying that Jesus is in everything. When He saved my earthly life from a possible death sentence by gangrene, He drew Cindy and me even closer together and stronger in our faith. I am using this ordeal to share my faith with those I would have never known without this experience. It has also drawn me closer to Jesus.

So, in the end, don't look at a trial as an oppression but rather an opportunity for so many blessings from Jesus! Because *God is good all the time,* and *all the time, God is good!*

# Reflections on Grief

# 11

# Love and Loss

## BARB

It was a typical September day in 1949 when I first laid eyes on Bob during our ninth-grade English class. The classroom was filled with the chatter of students, but amidst the many voices, Bob's shyness caught my attention. He sat a few rows behind me with his striking brown eyes; when he looked up at me to exchange a smile, it felt as if the world paused for a brief moment. Little did I know that this initial spark would ignite a profound connection that would shape our lives in ways we could never have imagined.

As the school year progressed, our friendship blossomed into something deeper. Then, as fate would have it, I found myself pregnant just before my seventeenth birthday. The weight of this revelation was overwhelming, but rather than face it alone, we decided to face it together. One afternoon, we nervously stood before a judge, pledging our lives to each other and stepping into the complex world of adulthood far sooner than we had anticipated.

Life as a young couple was challenging, filled with sleepless nights and the demands of parenthood. Bob worked tirelessly in various jobs, finally settling on driving a truck. I worked as a babysitter, juggling this part-time job while embracing the responsibilities of being a mother.

After many sacrifices and relentless determination, I finally earned my nursing degree, specializing in orthopedics—a profession that would become my passion throughout the years.

Our family soon grew with the arrival of three beautiful children: Kathi, Mark, and Karen, our youngest. With time, we built a comfortable life and decided to plant roots in a lovely neighborhood filled with blossoming flowers and friendly faces. The house we chose became a treasure trove of memories, each room echoing with the laughter of children playing, late-night conversations, and the comforting presence of family.

For sixty-one wonderful years, Bob and I walked hand in hand through the ups and downs of life. There were challenges, but our love was resilient and unwavering. We celebrated moments of joy, like birthdays and anniversaries, but we also faced sorrow and hardship together. Although I often believed our life was quite normal, I dreadfully underestimated the presence of suffering that hovered just out of sight.

In our family, the shadow of breast cancer loomed large. It started with my mother, who fought bravely, and several of my cousins followed suit, each battling their own fight. My own diagnosis in my mid-forties was a shock, but surgery granted me a second chance, allowing me to recover and return to my profession with renewed vigor.

However, just when I felt I could breathe again, the fates darkened once more. Bob was diagnosed with lung cancer at the age of seventy-seven, a diagnosis that shook our foundation. He underwent two major surgeries to remove portions of his right lung, braving countless radiation treatments, not considering the invasive chemotherapy that loomed as an option. The winds of illness continued to blow against us, yet we held tight to one another. Bob was later diagnosed with breast cancer—his doctor told us this was a rare occurrence for a man, but it felt like the universe was testing the limits of our endurance.

Our children, too, would face their own battles. Kathi was diagnosed with breast cancer shortly after I recovered; she fought tenaciously for nineteen long years, enduring treatment after treatment, supported by the love of her husband and her two beautiful children. I remember the look in her eyes—fierce determination paired with an underlying weariness as she navigated the relentless tide of her disease.

Mark, our middle child, once so full of life and energy, became another heart-wrenching story. He pursued his dreams, running a business with ambition and dedication, but he developed a troubling symptom: nagging difficulty swallowing. Eventually, he was diagnosed with throat and tonsil cancer, and the reality of his struggle was painful to witness. The bright spark that had once been Mark dimmed as he endured painful treatments, resorting to a feeding tube for sustenance, and his once cheerful laughter faded into a barely audible whisper.

In the autumn of 2013, I faced a most significant loss. Bob, after three arduous years of battling cancer, succumbed to the illness at seventy-nine. His absence left a void so profound that it seemed impossible to breathe. Each night after he passed, I missed the warmth he brought to our bed and the sound of his voice filling our home. He was my partner, my helper, my heart. I struggled with his absence, the emptiness echoing through our once-vibrant home. In the months that followed, the world felt gray and heavy.

As illness wreaked havoc on our family, I felt helpless but resolved to keep my faith alive. Prayer became my refuge, God's Word my strength and lifeline in a sea of uncertainty. My community at church was remarkable; they surrounded me with unwavering support. I clung to their kindness; the cards and notes sent my way proved to be a source of strength, their words lifting me when I felt I might crumble.

The grief did not spare me, as Mark passed away in November of 2023, followed by the loss of our beloved dog in February of 2024, who had been a constant comfort through our trials. Then, in May 2024, the unthinkable happened—Kathi, my brave daughter, left this world, leaving behind a heartbroken family.

Every loss felt like a blow that could have shattered anyone with fewer resources, yet I remained tethered to my faith, a quiet strength that endured amidst the chaos. I found some solace in the loving arms of my church community. Sunday mornings were filled with warm hugs and shared prayers, each encounter reminding me that I was not alone in my sorrow. I now have a basket overflowing with cards and notes of encouragement—a tangible testament to the love from friends and acquaintances alike. Each piece of paper tells a story of connection, compassion, and understanding.

I immersed myself in support groups at church, finding comfort in sharing my experiences with others who had also suffered loss. Through Bible studies and community gatherings, we became a tight-knit family, supporting each other with every burden we shared. Together, we encouraged one another, bridging the gaps of pain with a binding of love, reminding ourselves that loss might isolate us but also unites us in the most profound way.

As I reflect on my life at the age of eighty-nine, I recognize the intricate dance of love and loss that characterized my journey. Each memory etched within me is a testament to the beauty that arose from the struggles. With every hug I receive at church, every shared memory with friends, and every quiet moment spent in God's Word and prayer, I find the strength to continue moving forward, forever carrying the enduring love of Bob, my children, and the family I lost along the way, cherished and held deep in my heart.

Although pain and sorrow have filled my life, I have found an unfailing love with my Lord Jesus Christ. God's presence is so completely real on a daily basis that I experience joy beyond understanding. I trust His Word as it says in Deuteronomy 31:6: "Be strong and courageous. Do not be afraid or terrified, for the Lord your God goes with you; He will never leave you nor forsake you." John 14:27, as Jesus said: "My peace I leave with you; I do not give to you as the world gives. Do not let your heart be troubled, and do not be afraid."

At this time in my life, I genuinely experience the joy through suffering that I believe only the Lord can give, and I know it is something I experience almost daily.

# 12

# Emily's Story for His Glory

## CHUCK AND RENE'

## GOD AND FAMILY: EXEMPTION FROM PAIN?

### RENE'

Many years ago, I talked with a close friend about giving God everything, but we both added, with a smirk, "Well, everything except our children."

As new parents who faithfully attended church services on Sunday mornings, Sunday nights, and Wednesday nights, we knew that dedicating our firstborn child, Emily, to the Lord was not only expected but also the right next step to honor God and His wishes for our small family.

My husband, Chuck, and I were faithful in trying to raise our three children to love God and love others in words and deeds. We were extremely blessed to have generations before us who also loved God and loved others and encouraged us to keep on keeping on in our faith journey.

I felt that our dedication and devotion to God and the church would protect us from harm to our children. We were faithful in our church attendance, family time, scripture memorization, praying together at bedtime, serving in our home church, and we went on mission trips, tithing faithfully, and spending time in daily devotions. I genuinely believe that Chuck and I had a sense of "nothing bad will ever happen to us, *especially* not losing a child." Remember, Lord? Our family is "blessed," and we have honored you faithfully. Shouldn't we be exempt?

## Smith Clan: Perfect #5 | Chuck

My wife, Rene', and our three children, Emily, Caleb, and Zack, were known as the "Smith Clan." Our oldest was Emily, who was twenty-eight years old at the time of the accident and worked as an admissions representative for Spring Arbor University. Caleb was twenty-six and in his second year with the Michigan State Police, serving Jackson and Hillsdale counties while working out of the Jackson post. Zack had recently graduated from Spring Arbor University and worked in the Jackson area. All three kids were still single, and we were still doing many things together as a family, such as taking our annual end-of-the-summer camping trip to Young State Park in northern Michigan, where we had been vacationing together almost every summer for the past fifteen years. We had all been together in August before the accident, with unmarried adult children who still wanted to vacation with their parents. Rene' and I thought it was pretty special, to say the least, because we knew these days would not last forever. As we did the April before the accident, our three "kids" joined us in Florida for spring break.

We look back at these vacations with all five of us there and are so thankful for those times together. In hindsight, these two trips were among many little blessings of quality time and memories made together as a family before things would soon change.

The five of us attended the Jackson Free Methodist Church, where we had been going for all the kids' lives and our married lives. Rene' grew up in this church, and her parents and grandparents were practically founding members. Rene's sister and her family had also been attending for years. Many of our relatives are also in the area, and we would frequently get together for family birthdays and holidays. All that to say we were and still are a very close family.

So then, doesn't trying to be good Christian people and having a close family somehow exempt us from the problems and heartache the rest of the world experiences? I believe I developed that mindset early in my life, and it was still stuck in my head at some point five years ago when Emily's accident occurred. Losing our daughter was a huge loss, and it caused us to realize very quickly that nobody is exempt from loss and trauma in life. We will face it sooner or later, and preparing ourselves for it before it arrives is key. Our relationship with God and other believers is the foundation of this support.

## Church: Family | Rene'

I love being with people, especially children. So, attending church, working in the children's programs, and being involved in public education were all life-giving to me. My husband, Chuck, worked as a facilities director for thirty-four years at Somerset Beach Campground, where we had the privilege of being involved in the camping ministry. For many years, it was a blessing and a privilege to belong to our SBC family. Chuck and I were also involved with a small group Bible study for many years, but it disbanded when children and schedules took up all of our spare time. After the accident, when we were so vulnerable, some from our original small group, along with a few newbies, formed a new small group to help hold us together and support us spiritually, emotionally, and physically.

Before the accident, Emily taught a three-year-old Sunday school class, and our boys worked as volunteer leaders with our church youth group. Our youngest son helped lead our adult worship. All three of our children also served in many different capacities at our campground, from working maintenance alongside their dad to being camp counselors for many children.

From the outside, I would guess many would look at our family and say that our family had it all together. No fears, no struggles in marriage, no rebellious children, but they would be wrong, as we, like every family, had our share in these areas. Thankfully, we had a church family and our own family who loved us unconditionally, and they knew us well enough to speak truth into our souls, holding us accountable and challenging our behaviors and our faith while reminding us that God loved us. We were reminded that without Him, no one can survive evil in any capacity, including loss.

## Prepare the Way: God's Goodness | Rene'

By staying connected to our church family through the years, we were able to grow our faith under the leadership of some amazing pastors through their teaching and preaching. We were also engaging in meaningful worship with a team of musicians who would lead us into the heart of worship every week. Jason Engle was our pastor at the time of Emily's accident and had been Emily's youth pastor before becoming our lead pastor. Pastor Jason's sermons challenged us to give God our "yes" every morning before our feet hit the floor. Thus began a new journey of giving God my "yes" every day before my feet hit the floor. God was preparing the way for things to come.

Our church was also challenged to become better at reaching the lost in our community in Jackson, Michigan, by "loving God and loving others." Our baptism Sundays were in full swing, with new people giving their lives to Christ and sharing their testimonies. Our new theme was to share "our story for His glory." As a family, we grew in our faith and the time we spent daily with Jesus and His word. God was preparing the way.

My next-door teaching buddy always had worship songs blaring in her classroom every morning before the children arrived. One morning, she called me in to listen to her new favorite song, "Waymaker." I had not heard it, but after listening to the words, "Waymaker, miracle worker, promise keeper, light in the darkness," I was hooked. Even our worship team from church started playing this song often. God continued to prepare the way.

## CHUCK

Many months before the accident, our Pastor, Jason, had encouraged us to choose a single word that we felt God would have for us. It took me a few days to decide what that word would be, but one day, I was standing in our kitchen and looking at a wall hanging of a portion of Proverbs 3:5: "Trust in the Lord with all your heart." That is when I chose the word *trust*. Little did I know how much I would need to trust God in the coming months and years. I chose the word *trust*, but now I also claim the remainder of the verse as my life verse: "Trust in the Lord with all your heart, and lean not on your own understanding; in all your ways acknowledge him, and he will make your paths straight" (Proverbs 3:5–6).

## EMILY: INDUSTRIOUS, DILIGENT | RENE'

Em was feisty, loved hard, and laughed even harder. She loved her family with a mama-bear fierceness. She looked after her brothers, sometimes a little too closely in her brothers' opinions, but they knew their sister loved them dearly and would do anything to spend time with them.

Emily was a saver of everything that mattered to her! Letters from her campers, "encouro-grams" from past mission trips, old Birthday cards, and letters written to her from family and friends, special children in her life, and college besties. After her accident, I enjoyed reliving the moments through her eyes as I read through all of these saved cards, notes, and a plethora of other saved items. She was so thoroughly loved, and she loved others with gusto!

Emily spent years dealing with anxiety and self-doubt, and that led to doubting truths about God and His words. I am still not sure whether it was because she had struggled with past sins that made her feel like she was not worthy of God's forgiveness and unconditional love or that her anxiety allowed Satan to mock her and cause her so much inner turmoil. Although many tried to speak the truth to her about God's unconditional and forgiving love, she had a hard time forgiving herself.

As a parent, when you lose a child, you spend time looking back and wondering what you could have done or said differently. One thing I would have changed was the perfectionism, ranging from my looks of disapproval when she slipped off the pedestal that I had built for her, to many talks that were more condemning instead of listening and loving. I am now praising God that I no longer dwell on these lies that were being fed to me, and I am so thankful that God instead forgave me and has allowed peace to wash over my soul, which I never thought possible.

I believe this is why Em was known to love everyone, and I mean everyone, without any judgment. If she heard any words that anyone might consider judgmental, she would defend the other maligned person unswervingly.

Em knew that she needed to surround herself with believers to help strengthen who she wanted to be. She knew that she was not strong enough to fight for her convictions if she hung with the wrong crowd, so she attended two different Christian Universities and then ended up working for one of them in hopes of continuing on the path that would lead to a stronger and more dedicated relationship with Jesus.

Emily went on mission trips where she found out that loving God and loving others was exactly where her heart felt closest to God. She prayed with children, encouraged the workers, and loved everyone God put in her path. She often told me that she didn't think she would ever have children of her own and that she would be a loving aunty to her brothers' children as well as love on all of her cousins' children. She did not have a chance to meet her brothers' children, but she fully loved her cousin's children, all the children she counseled at camp, and those who came through her Sunday School class at church.

After the accident, people came out of the woodwork to share stories with Chuck and me about how Emily had loved them, giving them money for date nights with spouses and campers with whom she remained in contact years later. From family to friends to coworkers, she was a servant-hearted and loving woman who wanted to love God wholeheartedly, even when it hurt.

## November 21, 2019, 8:45 a.m. — The Accident | Chuck

Emily was traveling on business, running late, eating an apple, and using her cell phone when she ran a stop sign on a rural country crossroad at fifty-eight MPH in her little blue Ford Focus. She collided with a Ram Pickup truck coming from her right side and going equally fast but was blinded by a house and trees, keeping them from seeing each other's approach to the intersection. At that speed and the force of the impact, Emily and her vehicle were launched over sixty feet into an adjoining bean field. Emily was buckled in, but the force of the impact caused her head to strike the dashboard, console, and side door, causing severe head trauma and brain swelling, along with other non-life-threatening injuries.

## November 21, 2019, 9:15 a.m. — The Call | Rene'

I was in my classroom when I received a call from the hospital asking if I had a daughter named Emily. My heart stopped as I was gripped with fear and shock, but I praised the Lord for a few seconds. I grabbed my coat and car keys, and as I ran out of the classroom, I yelled to my assistant that I had to leave right now because my daughter had been in a serious car accident.

As I ran across the parking lot toward my car, I shouted out loud to God, "I love you, I trust you, and I will still give you my yes." Those three phrases were repeated between quick phone calls to my husband, boys, parents, and father-in-law. (To this day, I am unsure how I managed all those calls, but I could still keep my car on the road. Oh, wait, yes, I do: thank you, Lord!) I wasn't able to find a parking spot on the first floor of the emergency room parking garage, so as I continued up to each floor, unable to find a spot, I just kept asking God to grant me a miracle: "Please, Lord, don't let her die before I get to see her." As I look back at my request, I see now how God was preparing my heart for the possibility of saying goodbye.

I soon found out that I had gone to the wrong place to find Em, so thus began my same request, speaking out loud, asking God to allow me to see my daughter alive. For the second time, I went to the wrong place—the wrong fourth floor in the wrong tower of the hospital. As I felt as if I was beginning to fall apart with no strength left in my legs from shock, I came back down the elevator only to see the answer to my prayer: one of the parents of a child (Nurse Jenn) from Emily's three-year-old Sunday school class who worked at the hospital. She was standing there, looking for me. Jenn's sister was also my boss; she had informed her about the accident and had asked if she could look in on me. I literally fell into her arms while she held me so tight to keep me from falling. As we walked, she continued to hold me up, and she prayed with me. Jenn was able to get me to where I needed to be as fast as possible.

Nurse Jenn (we have now dubbed her "our angel") was instrumental in helping us understand what the doctors were saying, staying by our side and being the go-between for the next couple of days. Jenn would talk with the doctors and nurses for updates, and then she would come and relay in layman's terms to our family and the growing number of extended family and church friends.

## Our Boys

After a few years under his belt as a state trooper, our son Caleb was awakened from a dead sleep by his brother Zack. Caleb had worked a night shift and turned his phone off. I guess I hadn't made the seriousness of the situation clear in my quick phone call. They later said they just understood that Em had been in an accident. So, instead of panicking, Caleb called dispatch to ask about the accident, and they informed him that there had been one, and the victim had been transported to the hospital. They both got ready and went to the hospital to check on their sister. It wasn't until they arrived that they were hit with the fact that their sister was in critical condition. The looks on their faces broke my heart.

## Chuck

I never received a call from Rene'. I was on a mower and vacuuming fall leaves at the campground when I was approached by a crying co-worker telling me that Emily had been in a serious accident and that I needed to get to the hospital ASAP. That kind of news is a serious gut punch. I prayed and cried out to God the whole way to the hospital, twenty-five minutes away, not knowing exactly what I was headed for or the extent of what had happened. I was truly in total shock. I prayed a lot of different prayers as I drove like a maniac and pleaded with God on my daughter's behalf. But as I neared the hospital and would soon know what was happening, I prayed for God's will and that whatever happened and whatever the outcome, He would be in it all and help us through whatever was to come, and I trusted Him. Even as I write this chapter, five years after the accident, God is still in it and helping us through it.

## November 21, 2019: Emily's Condition

From a post by Emily's friend, Olivia Sanders, on Caring-Bridge:

> Today, our sweet, joyous friend Emily was in a serious car accident that resulted in a broken pelvis, collapsed lung, lacerated kidney, lacerated forehead, and severe bleeding of the brain. There is brain function; she responds to stimuli but is still unconscious. If the brain swells, the result is not good.

## Fourth Floor: A Glimpse of Heaven | Rene'

Watching our boys in action as they prayed and blessed others during our time of waiting gave their dad and me quiet confidence that they were ready for whatever God had in mind for their sister. As more people kept filing into the fourth-floor lobby, the boys would each take turns standing and greeting and loving on those who were hearing the details of the latest update, and some just needed to be held. Chuck and I were physically and emotionally exhausted, so we had time to sit and observe the scenes unfolding. Em's work family showed up with food, hugs, and willingness to begin a CaringBridge page to help keep others informed of Em's condition. Our boys also posted on Facebook and the CaringBridge page to inform our prayer warriors throughout the country and beyond how they could be praying.

## November 21, 2019 (From a Facebook Post) | Zack

> Lord, we believe in You. We trust You are who You say You are and that You can do miracles! Right now, we are asking for a miracle that Your healing hand will not only keep Emily here but that You will heal to *completion*! We know that You *are* moving; we have seen it already, and Lord, we thank You for what You've done through this already. The impact that Emily has had is evident in how many people have rallied around her in prayer! Thousands, at this point, are praying on her behalf! Thank You, Lord, for their faithfulness in stepping out in faith! We ask for peace as we wait for You to move, a peace that passes our own understanding! A peace that no matter what happens to Emily, she is Your child, and You have her! Lord, we have no control. We relinquish it all to You, Amen!

## Rene'

I have strong memories of the fourth floor, and all of them are good!

- My mom is sitting with her Bible open on her lap, willing to share a verse or a prayer with whoever needs it.

- The eyes of the precious family were full of love for us as they would wait for us to emerge from Em's room to hear the latest update, which was so full of love, compassion, and tears.

- My pastor, who was willing to go to a local store and get me some eye patches so I could sleep in the waiting room, to a dear friend who showed up (with a brand new, fuzzy blanket) just as my body was beginning to shake and my teeth to chatter from the shock.

- The dear friend who stayed awake through the first night quietly sat beside me, only speaking when necessary. When I started to talk out of control about what the future would hold without my daughter, she quietly said, "Rene', just one moment at a time. Take a deep breath, and ask God for enough strength to make it through the next moment."

- The arrival of family from out-of-state and Em's dear friends from out-of-state who had driven long distances led to the joining of old friends and family greeting, hugging, crying, and yes, even laughing together.

As we took over the floor waiting room with a constant of fifty or more people throughout the day, the food continued to be delivered to feed those who had come to minister to our hearts. On more than one occasion, the nurses would see our immediate family retreat back into Em's room, and they would ask us if we wanted them to clear the fourth floor so we could have some space and peace. We adamantly said, "No!" These people were our lifeline, our support system, and it truly felt like we were getting a small glimpse of Heaven.

## November 22, 2019: Saying Goodbye — See You Later | Rene'

As the hours rolled by, the reports became increasingly less hopeful. We finally had the final talk with the doctors, where they gave us the choice of what next steps we needed to take with our Em. As the four of us stood around Em's bed, the tears flowed as we all knew it was time to let her go, and ironically, we even felt a peace about saying goodbye.

We finished listening to all the medical reasons as to why we should stop life support, and we knew it would be a good decision, but it was just so heartbreaking. Our family did not feel complete. The hole was growing larger, and the emptiness was settling in as we had to say goodbye. We wanted to finish hearing each other's hearts without the presence of doctors and everyone else on the fourth floor, so we wound up in a small alcove just outside Em's room. We fell into each other's arms, and a wail that came from deep within each of us escaped all of our souls.

When we felt we had nothing left, our son Zack began to pray, and wow, did he pray! Loud and strong, full of faith over fear, full of wisdom beyond his years, and full of peace in the midst of the storm. We found out later that right across from us in the adjoining hall was the other person involved in the crash. Although we had already been praying for him, too, we hoped they knew we loved them and had prayed for his healing as well.

We were then given the option to choose life for others by signing papers and allowing the "gift of life" to harvest Emily's organs and tissue. We had all heard about organ donation and had applauded others when they had chosen it for their loved one, but when it hit home, and it came to signing papers for our daughter, our own flesh and blood, that word was almost too hard even to repeat because it wasn't just organs and tissue; it was our Em.

## November 22, 2019 (From a CaringBridge Update) | Caleb

> I type this with a heavy heart. Our family has made the very difficult decision to no longer have the MRI performed for fear of hurting Emily further and possibly jeopardizing the chances of using Emily's organs to bless other people in need. All family and friends here at the hospital have said goodbye to Em and have released her into Heaven's gates. Soon, Emily will walk with Jesus and hug my Nana and other relatives. Soon, she will be healed. Soon, she will be free.
>
> The family has decided to donate all of Emily's organs and tissue to those who need them to sustain life. In a sense, Emily is blessing others as she departs us. This process of donating the organs is going to be tedious, so for everyone who has been

following Em's journey and praying for her, we ask you now to begin to pray for the doctors who are going to be completing this careful process. There are a few last tests to complete before this process begins, so we expect Em to pass sometime this evening or tomorrow morning.

Thank you to everyone who is praying. God is good, and we trust Him during this and believe He will use Emily's story for His glory!"

## NOVEMBER 23, 2019: THE DAY EMILY PASSED

Rene's sister, Karen, wrote in a post:

> Over the past few days, our hearts have been broken, our eyes swollen and red with weeping, our minds filled with unanswered questions, and our arms void of our sweet Emily. But in the past few days, our hearts have also felt peace, our spirits refreshed, our love for the Lord renewed, and our arms filled with love, care, and hugs from many friends and family. We have seen love in action, God at work, and hearts changed. Emily set an example as a servant, caretaker, encourager, and friend who loved God and others. Her sense of humor, love for fun, smile, and laugh were infectious. Every day, she made a difference in the lives of those she came in contact with. In life and death, God used her and will continue to use her story to make a difference.

# Going Home: Double Meaning | Rene'

We said our goodbyes on Saturday evening, November 22. On November 23, after two nights and almost three days of living on the fourth floor of the hospital, a small part of me (and I believe it was true of our now family of four) felt like we wanted to stay at the hospital where Em's body still lay in the hospital bed and was being kept on life support, waiting for when they would harvest her organs. However, we knew that it was time for us to return to our home, as Emily was soon heading for her eternal home, or maybe she already had.

Our house felt cold and empty, but within minutes, we also noted how clean it was. Someone had been there and had ministered to us by cleaning our home. One of the first of many, many times we would ask ourselves, "Why are we so blessed?"

Em's bedroom felt empty and quiet, where once it was filled with goofiness and laughter. Within hours of arriving home, our kitchen was again filled with laughter when some of our church family arrived to deliver enough food to feed an army or at least feed our family and visiting family for days. The delivery group consisted of dear friends who filled our kitchen with food, laughter, and goofiness, which may have been needed more than food (His Mercy never fails: another blessing).

The next day would be Sunday. I couldn't imagine being able to fall asleep that night, let alone have the physical and emotional strength to get up and attend church.

## NOVEMBER 24, 2019: THE MORNING AFTER EMILY PASSED

But God, in His goodness, allowed me to sleep soundly, as I believe He had also allowed the rest of our family. When I woke, I was refreshed. The sun was rising, and my devotional chair sat empty, calling me to sit and enter into holy communion with my Heavenly Father. I took out my devotional, *Jesus Always*, by Sarah Young, which I had been reading through the past year, and turned to November 24.

## NOVEMBER 24, 2019 (FROM A FACEBOOK POST)

> This is what I read this morning. Wow, God! You are soooo amazing, and why am I even surprised? Between the many messages, I have spent all morning reading and then re-reading this, wow! My heart is full, and I feel blessed beyond what I could have imagined! Thank you, God. I trust You, I love You, and Your ways are higher than my own! Em's story for your glory!
>
>> "RECEIVE JOYFULLY AND THANKFULLY the blessings I shower on you, but do not cling to them. Hold them loosely–ready to release them back to Me. At the same time, I want you to enjoy fully the good things I give you. The best way to do this is to live in the present, refusing to worry about tomorrow. Today is the time to delight in the blessings I have provided. Since you don't know what tomorrow

will bring, make the most of what you have today: family, friends, talents, possessions. And look for opportunities to be a blessing to others."

When I remove from you something or someone you treasure, it's healthy to grieve your loss. It is also important to draw closer to Me during this time. Cling to me, beloved, for your relationship with Me will never be taken away from you. Let Me be your Rock, in whom you take refuge. Often, I provide unexpected new blessings to comfort you and lead you forward. Be on the lookout for all that I have for you!" (from *Jesus Always*, Nov 24, by Sarah Young)

Then came the words from my other devotional book, *Jesus Calling*, also by Sarah Young.

Thankfulness takes the sting out of adversity.
That is why I have instructed you to give thanks for everything.
There is an element of mystery in this transaction: You give me thanks (regardless of your feelings), and I give you Joy (regardless of your circumstances). This is a spiritual act of obedience—at times, blind obedience. Those who obey me in this way are invariably blessed, even though difficulties may remain". (from *Jesus Calling*, Nov 24, by Sarah Young)

Tears filled my eyes as I knew God was asking me to still *trust Him for everything*. I wanted to be obedient, even if it hurt.

Our family went to church, and blessings were poured out on us through obedient people who ministered to our family through worship, sermons, prayers, and hugs, especially during the powerful worship time of singing. Two songs were sung that morning, "This We Know" and "Waymaker," the song that I had been introduced to just a few weeks prior by my teaching buddy. I felt that God had orchestrated that morning's service to bless our family and show us His great love for us. Our job was to continue to be obedient and trust His plan fully.

Each day was a gift for the next few weeks and months if we could make it through without folding over in tears. So many posts and cards were sent out, informing and loving on us and helping us carry the heavy load. A celebration of life was planned, trying not to interrupt Thanksgiving plans for people and yet not wanting to wait too long to hold the service.

## December 1, 2019: Celebration of Life — Hope | Rene'

As we met with our pastor a few days after the accident, every conversation concerning our daughter's death felt like we were in a dream. I felt like if someone were to punch me, I wouldn't even feel it. I just felt numb and went through the motions. Don't get me wrong, we felt God's presence with every step and decision we made, but sometimes it just felt like His hand lifted ours to sign papers, or His voice spoke up when someone from her bank or her work asked for confirmation of her death or other details. Thankfully, meeting with our pastor felt like coming home, a safe place to speak about our wants and wishes for Em's celebration of life. Thankfully, Pastor Jason took charge and talked us through what everything would look like, and all of the details of food, service, and worship would be done for us. We asked if our worship team could sing the two songs sung on our first Sunday back after Em's passing, "Waymaker" and "This We Know." And they graciously offered to be there for us.

On the evening of the Celebration of Life and visitation, I was overwhelmed by the number of people who showed up, many of whom I didn't have time to greet and thank for coming, which was hard for me, being the people person that I am. There are many we still hear from years later that we didn't even know were in attendance.

Leading up to the Celebration of Life, I believe God asked me to stand and say something before the service began. I had already learned that I needed to be obedient to whatever God asked me to say or write, but getting up and speaking at my daughter's Celebration of Life was a new ballgame. So, I gave myself an out and told our pastor that if I felt like I wasn't supposed to talk, then at the last minute, I would give him the signal that I would not be getting up and saying anything (I truly felt like God would let me off the hook with this request). As I sat on the front row with my husband and sons, the Lord nudged me again, so I knew I had to get up, no questions asked. Every time I tried to write down what I thought God would want me to say, I would emotionally lose control, and so I finally got the hint that God would give me the words as I needed them.

I still have no idea what I said. Still, I think I spoke from my heart and hopefully expressed our sincere gratitude for the outpouring of love and prayers that we had already received and what I knew would be a continuation of an outpouring of blessings to come. People came up afterward, thanked me for my words, and praised our family for the strength we showed in the midst of our loss. All I could say was, and I said it with a strong conviction *Not by our strength but by His mighty hand are we still standing, along with the mighty power in the prayers of many.* Our pastor recently said, "Prayer is the arm that moves the hand of God." The prayers were many, and God's hand moved in miraculous ways, and we were just grateful to be close enough to watch His mighty hand in action.

## Grief Happens: Grief Without Judgment | Rene'

Each day brought new gifts of love, encouragement, prayers, and verses sent by loved ones.

Each day, I spent time in the Word because I had to. It was life-giving to hear from God in a whole new way. I spent hours praying, giving God my yes, reading scripture, and crying. Lots and lots of crying. Sometimes, the grief was gut-wrenching, and I was bent over, hardly able to breathe. In those moments when I was almost sick to my stomach, and when the hole inside felt too deep to fill, I would literally cry out to God. I guess I liked to pray out loud, so I knew that God would be listening, even though I knew He was. During my grief, I would pray, telling God of my love for him, of my trust in His plan, and saying, "I know you see me, Lord, and I know you are grieving with me, and I know that you understand loss. Thank you for staying with me, loving me, blessing me amid my pain." By the time I was done praying out loud, my body would calm, and a peace that passed all understanding would envelop me, and I could sit back down and continue with my day.

I made a deal with the Lord. If I were to post or share anything on Facebook, I wanted it to be God-inspired and with a stamp of approval from Him. So, there were times that, amid tears, I would write out an entire post that I felt I had poured from my heart and soul and then asked God to bless it. Then I would push "send," and it would get lost and be unable to be found. I knew God answered that it was not to be posted and that I had instead just shared a letter with God alone. Other times, God would allow my messages to be sent. People would read them and comment; there were so many comments on some posts that I could not even respond to them unless God asked me to do so for a specific person. I had many, many new friend requests, and I also felt that God was telling me to accept them, so I prayed that God would use my words to bless them, too. Writing these posts became part of my healing, as I believe it was also for Chuck and the boys.

I also knew that I had to get back to my students at school for their sake, as it is hard for the very young to be without their teacher for very long. Change can be hard on them but also hard on me. I knew that I needed them. When I contacted my two bosses, who are also my dear friends, and let them know of my wishes to return, they set about preparing a small "grief area" across from my classroom in a storage area filled with food, water, memory verses, a soft blanket, and some Kleenex. They also kept a substitute teacher in my classroom in case I had to run out quickly, which happened often in the first few weeks. All I could say was, "Thank you, Jesus," and ask once again, "Why are we so blessed"?

## December 5, 2019: Missing Emily (From a Facebook Post) | Chuck

For those of you who were able to attend Emily's Celebration of Life, I hope you could sense the peace God has given us in the midst of this. Yes, it has been a roller coaster ride of highs and lows, and we know this will continue, but in the midst of it all, we also know that God has this! Yes, we are missing our Emily. Yes, there are emotional times. Yes, there is grieving, and yes, I am preparing myself for other stages of grief that are yet to come. But we will continue to trust Him even when it hurts. We are blessed, and we praise Him in this storm.

## Dec. 7, 2019: The Day We Emptied Emily's Apartment (From a Facebook Post) | Rene'

Emily took so many pictures from our front porch of the beauty of God's creation. Sunsets were her favorite because she was a night owl and not usually awake for the sunrises.

She said she felt closest to God when she experienced His amazing creation. This morning, when we are hooked up to a trailer and ready to head to her apartment, pack up her things, and clean them out, my heart rejoices at the view this morning (out our front window) of the sun rising in the East. God is still on the throne, and His grace is sufficient for each new day! Good morning, Lord. You have my "Yes" today, and I love you!

Upon arrival at Em's apartment, someone placed a bouquet of flowers in her parking spot. That was the first thing that brought many tears that flowed that morning. A few dear friends and family joined us in the emotionally heavy assignment before us. Going through what used to be called "stuff" now had an emotional connection and memory of our daughter. Although I felt like I was trying to stay strong, I mentioned that we would be taking most everything and donating it. A friend who was there wisely advised that all of it go home with us, and slowly, over time, we would go through it. She also urged me to keep Em's green fuzzy robe as mine. I am not a robe-type person, and I think I silently rolled my eyes. For many months after, I would bury my head in her robe and cry. Now, I wear it regularly and snuggle into my daughter's robe and just about anything else of hers I can fit into. (Em did not like for me to borrow things from her, so sometimes I have a little fun and talk to her about how I am wearing her shoes or clothes, and I'm sorry if it upsets her. And I laugh… or cry!)

## December 11, 2019: (From a Facebook Post) | Zack

> As I lay in bed, still trying to fully grasp all that's happened in the last couple of weeks, I go to old text messages I had with my sister, Emily. I decided to write her a text to heaven. It seems to be my "healing," in a way. Sort of like I'm talking to her about my problems, so here goes.
>
> Emily, it's been over two weeks since you've been in heaven. I miss you so much, I can't explain how I feel; it's like I'm expecting to see somehow you walk through the door all of a sudden or text

me to ask for pictures of Remi (his dog). The lack of communication is hurting me. I miss my sister and my friend. Man, how I wish God would just completely take the pain away that I'm feeling. I woke up last night sobbing, praying that this had all been a bad dream, but it wasn't. You are gone. I always made (jokes) that I would be the first one to go cuz I'm crazy and get myself into silly hijinks sometimes that would warrant a potential accident. Here I wish I could have been the one, or with you, so we could be there together. It's stupid, I know; I have a purpose here on earth, and I know you wouldn't want me to come with you so that I wouldn't be without you. You'd want me to go and live a life that pleases God and use this experience to glorify him as well; you were so special in that way. I wish I could just hug you one last time, text you about juicy details of what's going on in my life, and simply hear your voice. I never thought I'd be one of "those people" who would be going through something like this, and yet here I am, sending a text to your phone that you will never read. I love you so much, Emily, and I can't wait to see you again someday! Enjoy Heaven, save me a seat next to you at the enormous dinner table where we can make jokes again, and you can tell me all the cool places to hit up in Heaven! Love ya, sis!

## Grief | Rene'

When you experience loss, loss of any kind, I feel like God gives you glimpses into others' hurts and hearts in a whole new way. Before the accident, I always felt like I was a compassionate person. And yet now, there is a whole new level of compassion, and even hurt as I am, I want to pray without ceasing for whomever it is that is going through loss. When I think that I need to give some advice or share my journey, God stops me in my tracks, and He reminds me that prayer, listening, digging into His word, and holding on are what is needed most. Rick Warren said it best concerning the loss of his son: "The deeper the pain, the fewer words you use." Why? Because everyone's loss is different, so many circumstances are different, such as the loss of a parent, sibling, spouse, child, or children. Loss of a dream, a job, or a marriage all bring different levels of grief as well. So, there is no perfect formula for grief; there is only a perfect God we must trust for each step we take.

Romans 15:13: "May the God of Hope fill you with all joy and peace as you trust in Him so that you may overflow with hope and the power of the Holy Spirit." Give Him your "Yes," and obey whatever His call is on your life. Trust more and worry less. Remember that He has you and gives you enough strength for each day. Continue growing, digging into His word, and surrounding yourself with family, church family, and Godly friends who will speak truth, encouragement, and life into you. God prepared us in advance for the loss of our Em, so when the tragedy hit, we did not break. And God has and continues to carry us by using the hands and feet of others who speak love, life, and hope into our hearts. You are not guaranteed tomorrow, but you are given a clean slate daily to give God your yes!

*Reaching beyond the Pain*

# HER STORY FOR HIS GLORY | RENE'

A dear friend, Todd Holton, showed up at the hospital after we had all said our goodbyes on Saturday the 23rd. He had a bottle of anointing oil with which he said the Lord had told him to come and anoint Em.

The day before, he had prayed with Em and said he had felt a hand squeeze. So, when he showed up with oil, our family had a sense of "What is happening? Will this be a miracle? Will our Em wake? Is our faith strong enough to believe this could happen?" We were a mixture of emotions. As our immediate family, our pastor, and his son gathered around Emily's bed, Todd prayed over her for a miracle and then anointed her. Todd waited; we all waited, but the answer was no. Todd said he felt her spirit was already with Jesus, and we all agreed. We then changed our hearts and prayers to prayers of anointing her organs and tissue to save lives physically as well as spiritually for those who would be receiving Em's organs. We prayed for the recipients, and we prayed for the others involved in the accident. We prayed for divine intervention for everyone and anyone to come and know the Savior as Em did.

I had my own added wishes, which I voiced to my husband almost sheepishly, believing I was possibly asking too much of God. But I prayed that at least one of the recipients would be a child. Since Em loved children, I desperately wanted a child to receive a new life physically as well as spiritually. If it wouldn't be too much to ask the Lord, we would have a chance to meet.

## December 18, 2019: One Month After the Accident (From a Blog Post) | Chuck

Our prayers for healing were not answered as we had hoped, but God's plans are higher than ours. Emily's passing was no surprise to God. He has used it already and will continue to use it in the future. How, you may ask? Let me tell you some ways God has already been working as a direct result of Emily's situation and story.

First, it called people to prayer. Lots of people. Social media and the internet get the news out quickly. Some may have thought our prayers were not answered. But who says they were not answered? Maybe not in the way we hoped for, but if we are praying like we should be, we are praying for *God's will*, not our own, and then we have to trust Him, either way. He may not have healed Emily as we would have liked, but I can't say it enough, and I believe wholeheartedly that *we have to trust Him*. I wish we had kept track of all the specific instances we have heard of that directly resulted from Emily's story so far. People have come to know God for the first time due to this. People have turned their lives around and decided to make changes for the good, including a closer relationship with Jesus. People have once again been forced to consider the briefness of this life on earth and have been reminded this world is not our home but merely a drop in the ocean of eternity, and then they have evaluated or reevaluated their spiritual condition. People have grown closer to each other as they have leaned on each other for support through this tough time. People have mended relationships that were broken. People started to pray again when they had given up on prayer. People started going to church again when they gave up on church. And people received new hope in life through the gift of organs and tissue. I trust there are many more that we are unaware of. I praise God for how he can take death or any bad thing that occurs and bring about renewal on many levels, but ultimately renewed life is suitable for His Glory!

Inwardly, as a dad losing my daughter, I am still reeling and trying to come to grips with the whole thing, as are Rene' and the boys and our extended family and close friends. I know we have all had our moments. As Christians and believers in God's sovereignty, we all know without a shadow of a doubt that God has a plan, and somehow, this was part of it. *We really do trust Him!* But humanly, we grieve in our weaker moments while trusting God's sovereignty. We mourn the loss of a very special and beautiful daughter, an only sister, an outgoing granddaughter, a beautiful niece, a joyful cousin, a crazy co-worker, a good friend, or the energetic and vibrant personality that brought life to those around her! The reality of the situation comes in waves, and the finality of our relationship here on this earth with our beloved Emily is staggering. I just plain and simply miss her immensely. I don't know how else to say it. And I feel it physically. I have an ache in my chest that I can't get rid of.

As I sit here thinking about everything that has happened in the last month, I realize that maybe I'm still in shock. I don't know. I've never been through something like this before.

And now, as I write this chapter, five years after the accident, I was definitely in shock for quite some time, maybe even slightly depressed for a time. Some say it is denial, but I was not really denying the facts but instead feeling the effects of being deprived of a daughter. It has taken time to adjust, and there are those moments when I feel like it can't be real, but I know it is. I am beginning to believe, and as we have been told by those who have been there, we will never totally adjust but will *always* feel the loss. I recently heard someone say, "Grief is a chronic illness; the moment you get it, you have it for life."

But this I know: I will continue to trust God through it all.

## December 21, 2019: (From a Facebook Post) | Caleb

It's hard to believe it's already been a month since your crash. I miss you so much, Em. Wish I could hear you call me "Cabe" one more time. Wish I could hear one more goofy joke.

I know heaven is awesome, and your story is changing lives (which I am so thankful for), but your little bro is still hurting and could use one last Emily hug right now. I love you, Em, and miss you like crazy.

## December 23, 2019: One Month After Emily's Passing (From a Facebook Post) | Rene'

One month ago, our Emily was ushered into the arms of Jesus! Again, God showed up during my time with Him this morning. About a year ago I was having a very rough year at school. I began to read in my "Jesus Calling" devotional. The opening statement was, "I AM WITH YOU, I AM WITH YOU, I AM WITH YOU." As I cried, I breathed a prayer of Thanksgiving to God, who is present, offering His strength, direction, comfort, peace, and hope. Today, I got to the bottom of my devotion "Jesus Always," and there were those three words once again. I AM WITH YOU!! Then the Bible reading, along with it, took me to Matthew 11:28, "Come to me all who are weary and burdened and I will give you rest." He not only is giving me rest, but He is lifting me and strengthening me to keep on keeping on! We serve an almighty God!

My dear friend made a shirt for me yesterday with the words to the song she sent me two weeks before Em's accident. For those two weeks, I woke every morning with that song running through my head and encouraging me to say "YES" to Jesus before my feet hit the floor. It was just one of the many ways God prepared me for what would come. The song is: "Waymaker," "miracle worker, promise keeper, light in the darkness, my God, that is who you are!"

Keep pressing into Jesus. He is the reason for this season and for life eternal!

## January 20, 2020: (From a Facebook Post) | Rene'

God shows up. Em had some scripture memory cards taped to her bathroom mirror at our house. They had been there since she moved out and into her apartment three years ago. I took them down back in September before the accident, as I was remodeling the bathroom. Thus began my journey of adding my own memory cards to hers and beginning to memorize some of them. This morning some of these verses just leaped out at me, and I really needed to be reminded of them. As we continue to say, and especially since Em's passing, when something is not working out as we had planned, "It must be God's plan, so don't sweat it." Like one of our current questions, "Why wasn't her heart harvested too?" To the little things, like I lost one of her earrings that I loved while wearing it yesterday. We must stop and remind ourselves that His ways are higher than our own. After my devotions, memorizing scripture, and once again saying YES to Jesus, I got up from my chair, and there was her earring on the floor in front of the tree where Em's picture still hangs. "Yes," I cried. God is so, so, good, and then, to top it off, there was the beautiful sunrise, a reminder to me once again that God is in control. Phil. 4:6, "We do not need to be anxious about anything, but by prayer and petitions, with THANKSGIVING, present our requests to God." And here is the kicker, and the promise, Phil. 4:7 "And the peace of God which transcends all understanding will guard your hearts and minds in Christ Jesus." Nope, I don't understand it all. Why the blessings, why the pain, why the forgiveness, why the grace? But GOD SHOWS UP when we are obedient to seek Him and spend time in His word.

## February 4, 2020: (From a Facebook Post) — Loss vs. Love | Rene'

Yesterday was a rough day! My stomach ached, and my throat was tight! Every step with a smile on my face was difficult! Some days are like that. No reason I can attach to why that day was tougher than the day before. Then God reminded me: look around you. So, many people dealing with loss. Loss of a dream. Loss of a friendship, or relationship, or an illness that changed their life!

Everyone deals with loss in his or her own way. But truly, there is a right way. One that brings peace instead of more pain. One that takes away that ache in your stomach or turns your eyes back to the only true answer.

My husband spoke truth into my heart last night by turning me back to our sovereign Savior to trust in His plan and, ultimately, His grace and love that I cannot even fully comprehend.

And then this morning's devotion from *Jesus Calling* again:

Bring Me Your Weakness, and receive My Peace. Accept yourself and your circumstances just as they are, remembering that I am sovereign. Do not wear yourself out when analyzing and planning. Instead, let thankfulness and trust guide you through this day; they will keep you close to Me. As you live in the radiance of My Presence, My Peace shines upon you. You will stop noticing your weak or strong feelings because you will focus on Me. The best way to get through this day is to get through it step by step with me. Continue this intimate journey, trusting that your path is headed for heaven. (from *Jesus Calling*, Feb. 4, by Sarah Young)

Thank You, God, for loving your children!
*Your LOVE conquers our LOSS!!*

## OCTOBER 2020: GIFT OF LIFE — NEW LIFE | CHUCK AND RENE'

It wasn't until October 2020, almost a year after Emily's passing, that we made our first contact with a Gift of Life recipient. It had taken us a while to realize and bring ourselves to go through the process of "consent and release of information," which would authorize the exchange of confidential information between the donor family and the transplant recipient, or in this case, the recipient's parents.

The first person to contact us was a young mom named Grace. As we opened her letter, I (Rene') fell to my knees in tears at the goodness of God, who answered my request. Grace was the mom of a precious baby girl named Tillie, who received a portion of Em's liver. Tillie had been born with a life-threatening liver disease called biliary atresia.

After one failed attempt at a transplant, when the call came to them on the day we said goodbye to Em, Tillie's mom and dad began their journey to the Cleveland Clinic filled with a mixture of emotions.

Tilli's surgery was successful, and with that point of contact in October, a beautiful relationship between Tillie and her family and ours began. Many FaceTime calls, singing songs, and reading stories to Tillie. "Tillie girl" became our lifeline to Emily until February of 2022, when Tillie got COVID-19, which led to other lung complications. Chuck and I finally were able to journey to Oklahoma and visit Tillie, who was now on life support. We had the gift of meeting her whole family and her doctors and had the blessing of praying over them. Tillie went home to Heaven on Feb. 22, 2022. We believe that she not only woke in the arms of Jesus but that Em was also there waiting for her.

Em had a special love for three-year-olds, and Tillie turned three the December before she passed. We are so grateful for this precious family that God put into our lives, and we continue to stay in contact with them. We even had the absolute joy of visiting them in Oklahoma this past summer (2024).

God is moving and working in Grace and the rest of her family. We have seen lives rededicated, first-time commitments, the gift of another child, and even marriages restored. We and Tillie's parents have lost a daughter now, so there is a connection of sharing grief but also sharing joy, promises, encouragement, and prayers for each other.

Chuck and I continue to pray that many will come to know Jesus because of Em's story and because of God's story—this story of God's grace and love, even in the midst of grief.

> May the God of Hope fill you with all joy and peace as you trust in Him so you may overflow with hope and the power of the Holy Spirit. (Romans 15:13)

Give Him your "yes," and obey whatever His call is on your life. Trust more and worry less. Remember that He has you and gives you enough strength for each day. Continue growing, digging into His word, and surrounding yourself with family, church family, and Godly friends who will speak truth, encouragement, and life into you. God prepared us in advance for the loss of our Em, so when the tragedy hit, we did not break. And God has and continues to carry us by using the hands and feet of others who speak love, life, and hope into our hearts.

You are not guaranteed tomorrow, but you are given a clean slate daily to provide God with your "yes!"

#emilysstoryforhisglory

# Final Reflections

# 13

# Closing Thoughts

As Viktor Frankl, a Holocaust survivor, has said, "Suffering ceases to be suffering at the moment it finds meaning."[1]

If you live on this earth, you will encounter pain at some point in your life. Some pain is minor, and some is intense. Sometimes, it may last for only a few moments (as when you stub your toe), but at other times, it may last much longer.

According to the Mayo Clinic, chronic pain is any pain that lasts more than three months.[2] For those of us who live with this kind of pain, we realize that it can last for weeks, months, or even many years, and unfortunately, for some people, their pain can even last for their lifetime. I have personally struggled with chronic pain for forty-five years. I have continually searched for answers that would lessen my pain and possibly provide some relief.

If you are someone with chronic pain, you are not alone. The CDC reports that "51.6 million Americans suffer from Chronic Pain. People in the US suffer daily with life-altering pain."[3] But there is hope; the Mayo Clinic states, "Doctors, scientists, and researchers are constantly searching for answers for those of us who have found no relief."[4]

## Reaching *beyond* the Pain

No one knows your pain as you do, but those of us who suffer have many things in common, even if our type or origin of pain is very different. The age-old proverb "misery loves company" has often been repeated.

I don't believe anyone can fully share in our pain or misery, but it does help to talk with others who have experienced significant pain.

Talking with others who suffer may encourage us; other times, it may give us a new direction to seek help. Sometimes, it is simply enough to know that someone cares.

A look at pain and suffering is far more than mere medical statistics. Suffering comes in many forms: physical, emotional, and spiritual. Whatever type of suffering you may experience, it is helpful to realize that there can be meaning and purpose in it: The suffering of Jesus Christ is an example. In Dr. David Jeremiah's May 6, 2000 newsletter, he stated, "It was through suffering that Jesus Christ's incarnation [Jesus taking human form] was made complete. He chose to come to us so that He might become a merciful and faithful high priest in service to God."[5]

Why should we expect anything less for ourselves if Christ was made complete through suffering? One of the key points in Dr. Jeremiah's comment is that Christ was in service to God. He was part of God's plan, and so are we. He suffered deep anguish so that He might sympathetically identify with our needs and restore us to a right and holy relationship with our Father God through salvation.

Chris Teigreen wrote in his devotional book: "Just as the cross of Jesus revealed the character of God within Him, so does the fire of trial reveal the character of God within us. Superficial and real joy look exactly the same until the storm comes and blows one of them away. Nothing God gives us is

## Closing Thoughts

proven genuine until it is assaulted by the troubles of this world and the wiles of the enemy. It is the only way the authentic is distinguished from the superficial. It is the only way to come forth as gold. God's plan for all His people is trial by fire. It is the only way to burn away the flesh and reveal the Spirit. It is the only way to grow. No one has ever become a true disciple without perseverance, and no one has ever persevered without pain. Rather than looking for escape, look for the benefit of trial. Let endurance have its perfect result. Ask God what He's accomplishing and then participate in it willingly."[6] May we all, with God's help, "come forth as gold" in this world.

As you have been reading these stories, it is quite possible that you have been confronted with some of your own pain. Whether it is physical, emotional, or relational, pain can deprive us of peace and rob us of joy. If that is where you find yourself today, then I encourage you to turn to Jesus and ask for His help in reaching beyond your pain. In my experience, no emotion is so strong that His Spirit cannot help you. Just writing those words fills me with gratitude for the freedom and healing He has brought into my life and that He offers to each of you. At times, I have found it helpful to be reminded that God has a plan for each of us. In the words of the prophet Jeremiah: "For I know the plans I have for you, declares the Lord, plans to prosper you and not harm you, plans to give you hope and a future. Then you will call on me, and come and pray to me, and I will listen to you. You will seek me, and find me when you seek me with all your heart" (Jeremiah 29:11–13).

Please remember, Jesus does not condemn us. Instead, He came to restore us. His resurrection declares peace over our fear, offers grace and forgiveness from our sin and shame, and provides joy in place of pain and sorrow. This is a forever promise! God doesn't erase the memory of our pain, but He will set us free from the bondage that it can bring. In Revelation 3:20, we are reminded that Jesus Christ seeks out every one of us. He is standing at our heart's door, eagerly waiting to be invited in to help us face every challenge that comes our way. If you have never done so, I encourage you to call out to Him with a simple, heartfelt prayer such as this:

> Heavenly Father, I come to you in the name of Your Son, Jesus. I'm praying because I want a personal relationship with Jesus as my Lord and Savior. Help me to embrace Him as Lord over my life. I confess that Jesus is Lord, and I believe that You raised Him from the dead. I'm claiming Your forgiveness for my sins. Please help me grow to understand the Bible and be able to use it as a guide for all areas of my life.

---

[1] Viktor Frankl, *Man's Search for Meaning*, Beacon Press, Boston, 2006

[2] mcpress.mayoclinic.org/opioids/how chronic pain works

[3] Center for Disease Control. Atlanta, Georgia

[4] Mcpressmayoclinic.org/opioids/how-chronic-pain-works

[5] Dr. David Jeremiah, *Newsletter*, Turning Point Ministries, 2000

[6] Chris Tiegreen, *Walk with God. One year Devotional*, pp. 64–65, Walk Thru the Bible, Tyndale House Publishers, Inc., Carol Springs, Illinois, 2007

# 14

# Encouraging Words

Life isn't about waiting for the storm to pass; it's about learning to dance in the rain.

— Vivian Greene

When you come out of a storm, you won't be the same person that walked in. That's what the storm is all about."

— Haruki Murakami

Strength grows in the moments when you think you can't go on, but you keep going anyway.

— Unknown

Don't pray for an easy life; pray for the strength to endure a difficult one.

— John F. Kennedy

Accepting pain can be difficult, it's just better than the alternative, which is to live in a state of perpetual suffering.

Reaching *beyond* the Pain

—Vidyamala Burch and Danny Penman

Joy is not the absence of pain or sorrow, it is the presence of Christ in the midst of pain and sorrow.

—Elizabeth Elliott

You may know about Jesus, but you will never know Him deeply until He comes to you in the midst of the storms of life.

—Greg Laurie

May the God of hope fill you with all joy and peace in believing, so that by the power of the Holy Spirit you may abound in hope.

—Apostle Paul (Romans 15:13)

Faith in God fills us with joy and peace that transcends our understanding. (Through the Holy Spirit, we find hope in the most difficult times.)

—Apostle Paul (Philippians 4:7 with my commentary)

www.ingramcontent.com/pod-product-compliance
Lightning Source LLC
Chambersburg PA
CBHW070155100426
42743CB00013B/2920